Robert N. Burrows
English Department
University of Wisconsin-Whitewater
Whitewater, Wisconsin 53190

25 JANUARY 1985

GOLDEN HART GUIDES
BATH

GOLDEN HART GUIDES

Bath
City & Countryside

Yvonne Whiteman

SIDGWICK & JACKSON LONDON
in association with Trusthouse Forte

The publishers gratefully acknowledge
the co-operation of Charles Greenwood
and the Bath City Council for their
assistance and advice

Front cover photo: The Great Bath
Back cover photo: Longleat House
Frontispiece: View of Bath from Prior Park

Photographs by the British Tourist
Authority, with the exception of
ps 6/7, 32, 37, 44/45, 48 by Paul
Watkins and p 24 (Mansell Collection)

Compiled and designed by Paul Watkins
Editorial assistant: Andrew Franklin

First published in Great Britain 1983
by Sidgwick & Jackson in association
with Trusthouse Forte

ISBN 0–283–98909–2

Photoset by Robcroft Ltd, London WC1
Printed and bound in Great Britain
by Hazell Watson and Viney Limited,
Aylesbury, Bucks
for Sidgwick & Jackson Limited,
1 Tavistock Chambers, Bloomsbury Way,
London WC1A 2SG

Contents

Introduction

'The prettiest city in the Kingdom'. This was Samuel Pepys' description of 17th-century Bath, then a city of taverns and bear-baiting, where public bathing was a free-for-all. What would he have said a century later, when Bath had put on its face and become one of Europe's most stylish cities, a magnet for fashionable society? His description would certainly have been just the same – for such is the quality of this extraordinary city whose surface is brilliant but whose substance is hard to define.

Visitors peering into the recesses of the Roman Baths or gazing at the splendour of the Royal Crescent cannot quite grasp how such a grand place was not at some time a centre of government or of some national institution. But this is the city's greatest illusion: it is a façade, a magnificent sham. Not that this reduces its significance as a unique architectural concept, the stage-set of a brilliant age. But Bath is essentially a pleasure city. It has been called the first Monte Carlo, the Royal Crescent an early form of condominium; such comparisons are no caricature for a city where self-indulgence – whether the curing of aches and pains,

the admiration of sights, or the exchange of scandal – has for centuries been the order of the day.

Though it may have the appearance of a European metropolis and is administratively a part of the county of Avon, in spirit Bath is a provincial Somerset town. Farming is a vital part of the local economy, and the city's agricultural links with the market towns of Frome, Trowbridge and Shepton Mallet are far stronger than its links with Bristol – despite the fact that the two cities are only twelve miles apart. Shepton Mallet's annual 'Bath and West' is the country's finest agricultural show, while the name 'Cheddar' is synonymous with the delicious nutty cheese first produced in the area around the village of Cheddar.

Geologically, too, Bath is a part of Somerset, positioned on the oolitic limestone belt which runs through the county and Cotswolds via Oxfordshire to Peterborough. Many of the limestone caverns riddling the area have yielded valuable prehistoric finds; the animal remains found at Wookey Hole, for example, date back 35,000 years to the beginning of the Ice Age.

The Bath vicinity also borders on Wiltshire – spanning the area once inhabited by the Beaker people. This race, named after the small stone beakers found alongside skeletons excavated at Priddy, Ashen Hill and Ebbor Gorge, arrived from the Rhineland *c.*2000 BC and left gigantic monuments to themselves in the form of stone circles at Avebury and Stonehenge. The stone from the Marlborough Downs used to build Avebury was the first natural resource known to have been exploited in the area; next to be used was the silver-bearing lead first discovered by the Phoenicians and mined by the Romans in the Mendips; then calamine, dug nearby during the 18th century. A hundred years later coal mining brought prosperity to the region.

Standing at the point where the Mendips, Cotswolds and Wiltshire Downs converge, Bath has been subject to a mixture of geographical and historical influences. But beyond this the city exists in its own right as a symbol of excellence, and of the need to re-evaluate and preserve. It is no accident that Bath is one of the biggest centres for antique-dealing outside London, and that people throughout the West Country and Wales come here for their more specialised shopping and collecting. Traditional crafts such as bookbinding, cabinetmaking and ironwork thrive in Bath, along with the more popular silversmithing and pottery.

The city has inspired a bewildering variety of inventions: the Bath Oliver, a plain health biscuit; its delectable offspring the Chocolate Oliver; the Bath Chair, an invalid carriage; the Bath Bun, a sugared currant bun; and the Bath Chap, a piece of pressed pork. It was in Bath that Sir Isaac Pitman invented shorthand, and that Sir William Herschel discovered the planet Uranus. A host of Bath-inspired literary works were spawned in the city's Georgian heyday and for some time afterwards: Richard Brinsley Sheridan's *The Rivals*; Tobias Smollett's *Humphrey Clinker* and *Roderick Random*; Christopher Anstey's *New Bath Guide*; Jane Austen's *Northanger Abbey* and *Persuasion*; and Charles Dickens' *Pickwick Papers*. The portrait-painters Thomas Gainsborough and Thomas Lawrence and the actress Sarah Siddons also made their names in Bath.

So much for the past. What of Bath present and future? Recently the city's shabby gentility has been smartened up in a new wave of cleaning and restoration; property prices are rising fast; every week a stylish new shop, restaurant or wine bar springs up somewhere; plans are afoot for a new international spa complex – all indications that Bath may very soon become a

Longleat

fashionable resort once more. The streets bustle with life; buskers play, Morris Men step out and a mild festive air prevails. This is Bath at its best – taken at a leisurely stroll to enjoy the perspectives, sounds and smells that make up this unique city.

While offering its own delights, Bath also makes an excellent base from which to explore the surrounding country. The historic cathedral city of Wells and legendary Glastonbury, together with neighbouring Cheddar Gorge, lie within a 25-mile radius; so too do the mysterious sites of Avebury and Silbury Hill, and the magnificent Longleat estate with its many attractions. A more ambitious motoring excursion crosses Salisbury Plain to one of the world's greatest prehistoric monuments – Stonehenge.

For those who prefer their pleasures closer to home, there are many walks to be enjoyed on Bath's surrounding hills, as well as river and canal boat-trips, and excellent amenities for sports. The American Museum is only a couple of miles outside the city at Claverton, while for railway enthusiasts the Museum at West Cranmore, home of the East Somerset Railway, is a must.

Details of all these attractions and activities will be found in 'The Best of the Region' section of this book, together with an outline of local festivals and events. The Gazetteer provides a round-up of the principal places of interest outside the city, while Bath itself is explored in two walking tours. It is hoped that the reader will find this a useful and comprehensive guide to the beautiful city and countryside of Bath and that they, like so many of their predecessors, will find 'the cure'.

The Best of the Region

excluding City of Bath (p.28)

A summary of the places of interest in the region, with opening times. The location, with map reference and description of each place, is shown in the Gazetteer. Names in bold are Gazetteer entries, and those with an *asterisk are considered to be of outstanding interest. (NT) indicates properties owned by the National Trust.

Castle Combe

Churches

Those listed here are specially worth a visit, either for the building itself, or for some special feature such as brasses, heraldry, tombs or wall-paintings.

Avebury St James

Babington St Margaret

BATH see p. 28

Bathampton St Nicholas

Beckington St George

Berkley St Mary the Virgin

Biddestone St Nicholas

Bradford-on-Avon St Lawrence

Bromham St Nicholas

Calne St Mary

Castle Combe St Andrew

***Chew Magna** St Andrew

***Chewton Mendip** St Mary Magdalene

Chippenham St Andrew

Claverton St Mary

Compton Martin St Michael

Devizes St John

Doulting St Aldhelm

***Downside Abbey**

***Edington** St Mary, St Katherine and All Saints

Frome St John

Glastonbury St John the Baptist

***Heytesbury** St Peter and St Paul

Lacock St Cyriac

Limpley Stoke St Mary

Marlborough St Mary, St Peter and St Paul

Meare St Mary

***Mells** St Andrew

Nunney All Saints

Orchardleigh St Mary

Potterne St Mary

Priddy St Lawrence

St Catherine's Court St Catherine

Shepton Mallet St Peter and St Paul

Steeple Ashton St Mary

Stockton St John the Baptist

Trowbridge St James

Warminster St Denys, Chapel of St Lawrence

Urchfont St Michael and All Angels

★**Wells** Cathedral, St Cuthbert

Westwood Manor St Mary

Widcombe St Thomas à Beckett

Historic Houses

Admission to most historic houses is between £1-2 (children half-price).

Avebury Manor
Apr-Oct, Mon-Sat & Bank Hol 11-6; Sun 1-6. Open fine winter weekends and by appointment. No dogs

Badminton House
Written enquiry only

BATH see p. 28

Bowood
Picture Gallery, chapel & grounds: Good Fri-Sep, Tue-Sun, Bank Hol & Oct Sun 11-6. Rhododendron walks: May/Jun (confirm). No dogs

Chalcot House
Aug, daily 2-5

★**Corsham Court**
Jun-Sep, Tue-Thur, Sat, Sun & Bank Hol 2-6. Rest of year 2-4. Closed mid-Dec to mid-Jan

★**Dodington House**
Easter & May-end Aug, daily 11-4. Sep weekends only, 11-4

★**Dyrham Park** (NT)
House: Apr, May & Oct, Sat-Wed 2-6; Jun-Sep, daily except Fri 2-6. Park: Daily 12-6 or dusk

Great Chalfield Manor (NT)
Easter-Sep, Wed 12-1 & 2-5; tours 12.15, 2.15, 3, 3.45 & 4.30

Horton Court (NT)
Apr-Oct, Wed & Sat 2-6 or dusk

★**Lacock Abbey** (NT)
Apr-Oct, daily except Tue 2-6. Closed Good Fri

Little Sodbury Manor
Apr-Sep by appointment

★**Longleat**
House & grounds: Daily (except Christmas Day) Easter-Sep 10-6, rest of year 10-4. Safari Park: Mar-Oct, daily 10-6 or dusk

★**Prior Park**
House: May-Sep, Tue & Wed 2-5; Aug only Mon-Thur 2-5. Chapel & grounds: Daily 11-4

St Catherine's Court
Open to parties by appointment Tel (0225) 858159

Sheldon Manor
Easter-Sep, Thur, Sun & Bank Hol Mon 12-6 (Garden) 3-6 (House)

★**Stourhead** (NT)
House: May-Sep, Sat-Thur 2-6 or dusk; Apr & Oct, Mon, Wed, Sat & Sun 2-6 or dusk. Garden: Daily 8-7 or dusk

Wells: Bishop's Palace
House, chapel & grounds: Easter Sat, Sun & Mon 2-6; after Easter until Aug, Thur, Sun & Bank Hol Mon 2-6; Aug, daily 2-6

Westwood Manor (NT)
Apr-Sep, Wed 2.30-6

Parks, Gardens & Wildlife

Admission to the gardens of historic houses is usually included in a combined ticket for house and garden. (See admission to historic houses above.) Where the garden can be visited separately this is usually about half the price of the combined ticket. The entrance fee for other gardens open to the public is usually in the range 30-50p (Children half-price or less).

BATH see p. 28

★**Bowood**
House & park. See *Historic Houses*

Broadleas Gardens
Easter-Oct, Wed & Sun 2-5

Corsham Court
House & grounds. See *Historic Houses*

*****Dodington House**
House & grounds. See *Historic Houses*

Dyrham Park
House & grounds. See *Historic Houses*

Holt: The Courts (NT)
Garden only. Apr-Oct, Mon-Fri 2-6

Horton Court (NT)
House & garden. See *Historic Houses*

Lacock Abbey
House & grounds. See *Historic Houses*

*****Longleat**
House, gardens & Safari Park. See
Historic Houses

Orchardleigh Park
Daily (no cars)

Prior Park
House & garden. See *Historic Houses*

*****Rode Tropical Bird Gardens**
Daily 10.30-7 or dusk

Sheldon Manor
House & garden. See *Historic Houses*

*****Stourhead**
House & grounds. See *Historic Houses*

**Westbury: Woodland Park & Phillips
Countryside Museum**
Daily 10-dusk

Castles, Ruins & Ancient Sites

Unless otherwise stated, these sites are
accessible at all reasonable times.

Alton Barnes White Horse, Adam's
Grave

*****Avebury** Avebury Circle
Prehistoric stone circle

BATH see p. 29

Bathford Brown's Folly
Mid-19th-c. tower

Battlesbury Camp
Iron Age hill fort

Beckford's Tower and Museum
Early 19th-c. folly
Apr-Oct, Sat, Sun & Bank Hol 2-5

Bratton Castle
Iron Age hill fort

Cheddar Cheddar Caves
Prehistoric caves. Gough's Cave, Cox's
Cave: Daily, 10-6 (10-4 in winter).
Jacob's Ladder, Museum, Waterfall:
Easter to mid-Oct, 10-6

Cherhill White Horse, Oldbury Castle

Doulting St Aldhelm's Well
Early Christian spring

Farleigh Castle
Medieval ruins
Times as for Stonehenge

*****Glastonbury** Glastonbury Abbey
Medieval abbey ruins
Daily 9.30-sunset

Hinton Priory
Medieval priory ruins
Apr-Sep, Wed, Sat & Bank Hol 2-6
Closed Sun

Knap Hill
Neolithic earthworks

Little Solsbury Hill (NT)
Iron Age fort

Marlborough White Horse

Meare Lake Village
Iron Age settlement

Milk Hill
Iron Age earthworks

*****Nunney** Nunney Castle
Medieval castle ruins
Times as for Stonehenge

Overton Hill
Prehistoric site

Pewsey White Horse, Martinsell Hill
fort

Priddy Priddy Circles, Priddy Nine
Barrows, Ashen Hill Barrows
Prehistoric site

Scratchbury Camp
Iron Age hill fort

Sham Castle
Mid-18th-c. folly

*****Silbury Hill**
Prehistoric earthwork

Stanton Drew
Bronze Age stone circles

Stockton Australian Rising Sun
Hillside monument

★Stonehenge Prehistoric stone circles
Mar 15-Oct 15, Mon-Sat 9.30-6.30,
Sun 2-6.30; Oct 16-Mar 14, Mon-Sat
9.30-4, Sun 2-4. Closed Dec 24-26

Wansdyke
Saxon earthwork

Wellow Roman villa sites, Stoney
Littleton Long Barrow

★Westbury White Horse

West Cranmore Cranmore Tower
Mid-19th-c. folly

West Kennet Long Barrow
Prehistoric tomb

Windmill Hill
Neolithic earthworks

Woodhenge
Late Neolithic site

★Wookey Hole Caves
Prehistoric caves
Apr-Sep daily, 10-6; Oct-Mar daily,
10-4.30. Closed Dec 25

Yarnbury Castle
Iron Age hill fort

Museums and Galleries

Avebury: Alexander Keiller Museum
Mar 15-Oct 15, Mon-Sat 9.30-6.30,
Sun 2-6.30; Oct 16-Mar 14 closed at 4

Avebury: Folk Life Museum
Apr-Oct, Mon-Sat 10-5.30, Sun 10.30-
5.30; Oct-Apr by appointment

BATH see p. 29

Beckford's Tower and Museum
Apr-Oct, Sat & Sun 2-5

Cheddar: Cheddar Caves Museum
See *Castles, Ruins & Ancient Sites*

Cheddar: Gough's Motor Museum
Daily 10.30-5 (sunset in summer)

Chippenham: Yelde Hall
Apr-Nov, Mon-Sat 10-12 & 2.15-4.30;
closed Sun and Bank Hol

**★Claverton: The American Museum
in Britain**
Apr-Oct, Tue-Sun 2-5; Bank Hol Mon
and preceding Sun 11-5

**★Devizes: Wiltshire Archaeological
and Natural History Museum**
Tue-Sat 11-1 & 2-5 (4 in winter)

**Devizes: Wiltshire Regimental
Museum**
Mon-Fri 10-12.30 & 2-4.30

Glastonbury: Abbey Museum
Daily 9.30-sunset

**Glastonbury: Somerset Rural Life
Museum**
Easter-Oct, Mon-Fri 10-5, Sat & Sun
2-7; Nov-Easter, Mon-Fri 10-5, Sat &
Sun 2.30-5

Glastonbury: The Tribunal
Mid-Mar to mid-Oct, Mon-Fri 9.30-
6.30, Sun 2-6.30; mid-Oct to mid-
Mar, Mon-Fri 9.30-4, Sun 2-4

**Lacock: The Fox Talbot
Photographic Museum**
Mar-Oct, daily (except Good Fri) 11-6

**Oakhill Manor Model Transport
Museum and Miniature Railway**
Apr-Nov, daily 12-6

**Rode: Min Lewis Pram and Toy
Museum**
By appointment only. Tel (0373)
830531

Shepton Mallet Museum
Mon, Tue, Thur & Fri 2-5; Sat 10-4

Warminster: Dewey Museum
Thur 6.30-8 pm; Sat 11-1 & 2-4

★Wells: Wells Museum
Apr-Sep, Mon-Sat 10-6, Oct-Mar 10-
4, Sun 2.30-5.30 (Jun-Sep only)

**Westbury: Woodland Park and
Phillips Countryside Museum**
See *Parks, Gardens & Wildlife*

**Wookey Hole: Wookey Hole Museum,
Lady Bangor's Fairground Collection,
Madame Tussaud's Store Room**
Times as for Wookey Hole Caves
See *Castles, Ruins & Ancient Sites*

Industrial & Rural Heritage

Avoncliff Aqueduct

Bradford-on-Avon Tithe Barn
Mar 15-Oct 15, Mon-Fri 9.30-6.30,
Sun 2-6.30; Oct 16-Mar 14, Mon-Fri
9.30-4, Sun 2-4

Chewton Mendip Chewton Cheese Dairy
Butter made 2 or 3 mornings a week. Shop open Mon-Fri 8-5, Sat 9-5, Sun 9-1 (Closed at 4 Jan-Mar)

Claverton Pumping Station
Apr-Oct, Sun 10.30-12.30 & 2-6. Pumping weekends as advertised

Devizes Flight of 29 Locks Kennet and Avon Canal

Doulting Tithe Barn

Kennet and Avon Canal Bath, Limpley Stoke, Avoncliff, Bradford-on-Avon, Devizes, Honey Street (Alton Barnes)

Limpley Stoke Dundas Aqueduct

Priston Mill
Easter-Oct, Sat, Sun & Bank Hol 11-12.45 and 2.15-5; weekdays by appointment

Shepton Mallet: Wootton Vines
Daily (except Tue & Sun)

West Cranmore East Somerset Railway
Apr-Oct, daily 9-5.30; Nov-Mar, weekends 9-4. Steam rides Sun & Bank Hol, Apr-Oct

Wookey Hole Wookey Hole Paper Mill
See *Castles, Ruins & Ancient Sites*

Famous Connections

Many famous personalities are connected with Bath and its region. Those associated with the city are shown in the **Bath section** (see p.30). Those identified with places outside Bath are shown below: details of their association will be found under the Gazetteer entries.

Alfred the Great Chippenham, Warminster, Westbury

Allen, Ralph Claverton, Sham Castle

Arnold, Dr Thomas Warminster

Beckford, William Beckford's Tower

Boleyn, Anne Little Sodbury Manor

Brunel, Isambard Kingdom Box

Churchill, Sir Winston Claverton

Coleridge, Samuel Taylor Wookey Hole

Elizabeth I Longleat, St Catherine's Court

Ethelred the Unready Corsham

Fielding, Henry Widcombe

Fox Talbot, William Henry Lacock

Henry VIII St Catherine's Court

Landor, Walter Savage Widcombe

Lawrence, Sir Thomas Devizes

Lawrence, T.E. Devizes, Heytesbury

Morris, William Marlborough

Penn, William Wells

Phillip, Admiral Arthur Bathampton

Pitman, Sir Isaac Trowbridge

Priestley, Dr Joseph Bowood, Calne

Sassoon, Siegfried Heytesbury

Seymour, Jane Beckington

Strachey, Lytton Chew Magna

Wolsey, Thomas Marlborough

Hotels & Historic Inns

†Non-residential inn
(THF) A Trusthouse Forte Hotel

Bath Avon
The Francis Hotel (THF)
Queen Square BA1 2HH
Tel (0225) 24257

This elegant 90-room hotel is part of Bath's priceless Georgian architectural heritage. Occupying most of the S side of Queen Square, it was originally six private residences built in 1723 by John Wood the Elder. In 1816 No 6 was briefly the home of the poet Shelley and Mary Godwin (author of *Frankenstein*). Partially destroyed by bombing in the war, the building was subsequently carefully restored.

Calne Wilts
The Lansdowne Arms
The Strand SN11 0EH
Tel (0249) 812488

A 16th-c. inn enlarged in Georgian times to cater for the stream of coaching traffic from London to Bath each 'Season'. Until 1925 it was part of the estate of the Lansdowne family of Bowood.

Cherhill Wilts
†*The Black Horse*
Cherhill, Calne SN11 8UT
Tel (0249) 813363

A red-brick inn built in 1765, *The Black Horse* brewed its own beer until 1939 and was regularly patronised by sheep-drovers who penned their animals outside while resting on the way to Marlborough.

Chippenham Wilts
The Angel
Market Place SN15 3HD
Tel (0249) 2615

Mentioned by Tobias Smollett in *Peregrine Pickle* (1751), this inn was popular with visitors flooding to Bath by coach in the 18th c. A large bow window was built so that the staff could see coaches approaching.

Corsham Wilts
The Methuen Arms
High Street SN13 0HB
Tel (0249) 712239

Originally a Tudor building, this inn was given a new frontage in 1805 after it had passed into the Methuen family. The stone doorposts of the entrance carry the traditional chequers sign used by tavern-keepers who were also money-changers.

Devizes Wilts
The Bear
Market Place SN10 1HS
Tel (0380) 2444

A famous and fashionable inn where in the 18th c. anyone who was anyone stopped for refreshment and a rest on the way to Bath, including George III, Jane Austen, Sir Joshua Reynolds and the actress Sarah Siddons. *The Bear* provided a foretaste of the social pleasures of Bath. The son of one of the inn's tenants was the famous portrait painter Sir Thomas Lawrence (1769-1830), later President of the Royal Academy. Traces of the old 16th-c. inn still exist, but the frontage is mainly Georgian.

Glastonbury Somerset
The George and Pilgrims
1 High Street BA6 9DD
Tel (0458) 31146

One of the few remaining medieval inns in England, *The George and Pilgrims* was built for pilgrims to Glastonbury Abbey in 1475. The Abbey was destroyed at the Dissolution in 1539 but the hospice or inn survived because, the story goes, from inside it Henry VIII watched the burning. It has a central archway and three-storey bays on either side with mullioned windows.

Marlborough Wilts
The Castle and Ball (THF)
High Street SN8 1LZ
Tel (0672) 52002

Standing on the colonnaded N side of the High Street, this attractive 30-room hotel – a popular touring centre – is an ancient inn behind its more modern façade. The timberwork of the 16th-c. building is still visible, having escaped the town's great fire (1653). In the 18th c. passengers from London to Bath often spent several days of respite at the inn after 12 uncomfortable hours on the stage.

Norton St Philip Somerset
† *The George Inn*
The Plain BA3 6LH
Tel (037387) 224

A medieval inn of great character, *The George* was built as a hospice by the Carthusian Priory of Hinton. The inn was used by Cromwell and his men during the Civil War. (See also Gazetteer.)

Wells Somerset
The Crown
Market Place BA5 2RP
Tel (0749) 73457

This late 17th-c. timber-framed building was once a coffee house. An 18th-c. Wells physician, Claver Morris, recorded meetings here with friends and patients, for it was a common practice in those days for a doctor to attend a coffee house where he could be consulted.

Sport and Recreation

Boating Boat trips are available in the Bath area from:

Widcombe Top Lock (canal) reached from Pulteney Road. Waterbus service to Folly Swing Bridge near Bathampton and return. Operated by the Kennet and Avon Canal Trust. Tel (0225) 31757

John Rennie wide-beam canal boat to Claverton Pump and Dundas Aqueduct and return. Tel (0225) 60717

Sydney Gardens (canal) reached from Sydney Road. Supper cruises on narrow boat to Bathampton and return. Tel (0225) 29644

Pulteney Weir (river) reached from Pulteney Bridge. On the River Avon *Scenic 1*, a 65-passenger launch, makes frequent trips upstream from Pulteney Weir to Bathampton Weir and back along some of the most picturesque reaches of the river. Tel (0225) 66407

Bath Barge Company's *Pride of Bath* travels downstream from Pulteney Weir to Saltford and Kelston and back, passing through the Avon Valley and several locks; in the evening it makes these cruises with a pub stop. Tel (0225) 319882

Bradford-on-Avon (canal) Regular 2hr trips to Staverton or Avoncliff from Frome Road Wharf and return. Operated by the Kennet and Avon Canal Trust. Tel (02216) 6135

There is sailing on the Avon at Saltford Marina, which has facilities for every kind of craft from motor launches to narrow boats. The Chew Valley Lake is used by the Chew Valley Sailing Club who organise races, regattas and other events.

The headquarters of the *Kennet and Avon Canal Trust*, which operates an information centre is at Devizes. Tel (0380) 71279. Canal trips are available from Devizes Wharf.

Fishing on the Bath stretch of the River Avon between Pulteney Weir and Newbridge requires a rod licence from the Wessex Water Authority (Tel (0225) 313500). Most waters in Bath are controlled either by the Bath Anglers Association or by Bathampton Angling Association.

There is good fishing on the River Frome, controlled by the Frome Angling Club. Glastonbury Angling Association fish the River Brue and its tributaries and further N, the Chew Valley Lake is becoming more widely known for its well-stocked waters.

In Wiltshire, there is splendid trout-fishing on the rentable northern stretches of the Wylye at Warminster, and some excellent coarse and trout fishing available in season on the Avon and Kennet rivers (for details of licences, contact the Wessex or Thames Water Authorities). At Woodland Park near Westbury only five rods are permitted at a time – which gives good opportunities for the lucky few who get there first. Bradford-on-Avon & District Angling Club rents and annually restocks some 25m of water, as do the Melksham & District Angling Association. The River Biss at Trowbridge and the Rivers Marden and Avon at Chippenham are easily accessible to anglers.

The Kennet and Avon Canal also offers fishing, especially at Devizes, Semington, S of Melksham and S of Marlborough. Devizes, Pewsey and Marlborough Angling Associations all have fishing rights over stretches of the canal and are pleased to issue visitors' tickets.

Golf Bath and Lansdown Golf Clubs both welcome non-members, and there is a Municipal Golf Club in Royal Victoria Park, as well as a putting green. Outside Bath, Saltford has a golf course in addition to its marina. Mendip Golf Club, a couple of miles N of Shepton Mallet, is regarded as the best golf club in the West of England. In Wiltshire, Chippenham and Kingsdown near Bradford-on-Avon both have courses, while the North Wiltshire Golf Club just outside Devizes at Arn Hill Down has splendid views out into Somerset. Further out, Marlborough has its own course.

Riding There are riding stables near Bath both at Weston and at Combe Down. The Mendips and their surrounding countryside offer good riding together with gymkhanas and point-to-point races, with principal stables at Shepton Mallet, Wells and Wookey Hole. In Wiltshire, there are a number of registered riding establishments in the Marlborough and Devizes areas, with opportunities for riding or pony-trekking.

Caving Caving is a growing sport in the Mendips, with many intriguing caves apart from the biggest centres such as Wookey Hole. There are several local caving clubs.

Further information on all these sports is available from the Tourist Information Bureau in Bath or other local tourist offices (see p.28), or from the Yellow Pages telephone directory.

Festivals & Events

Many colourful events, from village fairs and agricultural shows to international music festivals, take place in Bath and its region. Outstanding events are:

April *Great Badminton* Badminton Horse Trials

May *Bath* West of England Antiques Fair; *Glastonbury* Druid celebration of Beltane on Glastonbury Tor, Roman Catholic pilgrimage (last Sun)

May/June *Bath* Bath Festival; *Shepton Mallet* Royal Bath & West Show

June *Bath* Bath Round Table Carnival, Somerset County Cricket Festival; *Glastonbury* Church of England pilgrimage (last Sat); *Stonehenge* Summer Solstice; *Westbury* Westbury Festival

July *Bath* Floral Festival

August *Edington* Music Festival; *Lacock* Village Fair; *Melksham* Carnival; *Priddy* Sheep Fair; *Shepton Mallet* Mid-Somerset Agricultural Show

September *Frome* Cheese Show, Carnival; *Glastonbury* Glastonbury Tor Fair; *Shepton Mallet* Cheese Show

November *Bath* Book Week; *Shepton Mallet* Carnival; *Wells* Carnival

December *Marshfield* Boxing Day Mummers; *Stonehenge* Winter Solstice

Walks

Bath city environs
Bath is fortunate in that unlike most cities, it still has picturesque scenery within easy reach of the city. There are a number of pleasant walks in the area: some of the more beautiful or interesting are given below. These are, however, only outlines and the walker is recommended to follow an Ordnance Survey Map. **For walks in the city, see p. 31.**

Walk 1 Royal Victoria Park (short walk)
From Queens Parade, enter the park gates and follow Gravel Walk below the Royal Crescent. Cross Marlborough Buildings to Cow Lane, and through to Royal Victoria Park, Botanic Gardens and Fish Pond. Return via Royal Avenue/1½m

Walk 2 Sham Castle
From North Parade Road, cross Pulteney Road and under arch for footpath to canal. Right at the towpath to Top Lock and cross canal. Past Darlington Place and Cleveland Walk to Bathwick Hill and then left at The Priory for footpath to North Road. Take road opposite to Bath Golf Course and on up to Sham Castle. From here follow footpath N to Warminster Road and back to Bath/3m

Walk 3 Prior Park
From Holloway up steps opposite Magdalen Chapel to Beechen Cliff. Follow footpath past Alexandra Park and bear left to Alexandra Road. Right up Lyncombe Hill and left into Rosemount Lane. Right into Ralph Allen Drive and up to Prior Park. Back downhill and right into Church Street, Widcombe Crescent, and left down Widcombe Hill to Bath/3m

Walk 4 Canal to Bathwick Hill, Bathampton or circular tour. (This walk explores a part of the Kennet and Avon Canal)

To Bathwick Hill Join canal at Lower Lock in Rossiter Road (bottom of Pulteney Road). Walk under two bridges, climb steps and cross the lock. Continue left along towpath past Chapel Lock, Bridge Lock No. 9,

Wash House Lock No. 10, Abbey View No. 11, Pulteney No. 12 and Top Lock. Emerge from canal at Bathwick Hill bridge/½m

On to Bathampton Cross Bathwick Hill and down steps to join canal on right towpath opposite Sydney Wharf. At Cleveland House cross canal to tunnel on left towpath, below Sydney Gardens and on to *The George* inn at Bathampton/2m

On to Dundas Wharf and return to Bath Walk along towpath through Limpley Stoke Valley, past Dundas Aqueduct to Monkton Combe. Leave canal at Dundas Wharf, take footpath to Croft Road/Shaft Road junction and up Shaft Road to junction with Claverton Down road. Follow footpath opposite NW across Rainbow Wood and Prior Park to Church Lane, Church Street and down Widcombe Hill to Bath/8m

Walk 5 Little Solsbury Hill from Batheaston
From Batheaston High Street, turn left following signpost to North End. To the left, follow Little Solsbury Lane and footpath to top of Little Solsbury Hill. Return by same path/1½m

Walk 6 Brown's Folly from Bathampton
From Bathampton cross the canal bridge to St Nicholas' Church. E along Tyning Road and cross railway and fields to Bathford. Up Bathford Hill to Mountain Wood. Continue up to Brown's Folly and follow footpath S along Bathford Hill ridge. Cross Bradford-on-Avon Road (A363) to Warleigh Hill. By Conkwell Lane to Conkwell and right to Dundas Aqueduct. Up to Brassknocker Hill and join Claverton Down Road/6m

Walk 7 Saltford Marina from Newbridge
From Newbridge riverside walk to Saltford Marina. Take footpath E to Kelston. Cross A431 and E to Kelston Round Hill. Footpath N to Prospect Stile and continue SE to Upper Weston. Return to Bath/8m

Walk 8 Avoncliff to Bradford-on-Avon canal walk
From Avoncliff Station walk to the Kennet and Avon Canal towpath and E to Bradford-on-Avon. Leave towpath at the Tithe Barn and follow Frome Road over bridge to town centre/1½m

Railway Walks
Railway enthusiasts may enjoy walking the more accessible sections of the area's disused railways. From Brassmill Lane near Newbridge the old Midland Railway track, now converted for cycles and pedestrians, runs through open country to Bitton. The Somerset and Dorset, a railway loved by photographers and steam enthusiasts alike, can be followed in several places: through Lyncombe Vale (a footpath leads into the vale off Entry Hill); from Combe Down tunnel via Tucking Mill Viaduct and along below Midford Castle to Midford Station (where the railway crosses the Somerset Coal Railway, immortalised as the filming location of *The Titfield Thunderbolt*); from Midsomer Norton Station via Chilcompton and Binegar as far as Windsor Hill on the outskirts of Shepton Mallet; and from Pylle to Glastonbury.

Other Country Walks
The environs of the *Chew Valley Lake*, covering 1200 acres, are a delightful walking area, whether approached from Chew Magna, Chew Stoke, or from Hinton Blewett. Further south the *Mendip hills* provide some spectacular walks. At Burrington village a path leads up through Burrington Combe, a famous beauty spot. Not far from Wookey Hole lies Ebbor Gorge, carved out of carboniferous limestone, with coppiced woodland; the gorge is a nature reserve populated with badgers, buzzards, sparrow hawks and kestrels. Both ½hr and 1½hr circular walks start at the car park.

The base of the *Cotswold ridge* N of Bath is less dramatic, but has its own gentler charm. The fields between Chipping Sodbury, Little Sodbury Manor and Badminton Park provide some pleasant strolls. S of the A420 the lesser-known country between Marshfield and St Catherine's Valley is well worth exploring.

E of Bath the country changes again, falling away into the rolling downs and woodlands of *W Wiltshire*. Cley Hill near Warminster gives superb views of the area, while nearby Westbury has a number of walks cut through its 120 acres of woodland park.

At Devizes the *Kennet and Avon Canal* moves through a remarkable flight of 29 locks before passing through the town and making its way E. Walkers taking the public towpath can follow the canal through into the Vale of Pewsey, an area of great natural and historical interest. Wansdyke, the huge Saxon earthwork built to repel northern invaders, can be seen at various points threading its way through the Wansdyke hills – Tan Hill, Knap Hill, Milk Hill, Huish Hill and Martinsell Hill.

Immediately N of the A4 lies the southernmost point of *The Ridgeway*, probably the oldest path in Britain. The pathway (85m in all) begins just E of West Kennet, and there are numerous other tracks to follow nearby: from New Bridge to Silbury Hill and on to West Kennet Long Barrow; from St James's Church, Avebury to Windmill Hill; from the Stone Avenue at Avebury to West Kennet, East Kennet, over The Sanctuary at Overton Hill across the A4 and back to Avebury; and W to Cherhill Down with its Iron Age hill fort and White Horse. The chalk Marlborough downlands are famous for their wealth of flowers and for their ground nesting birds such as lapwings and skylarks. SE of the town of Marlborough lies *Savernake Forest*, a magnificent expanse of woodland 16m in circumference, including many fine avenues of beech originally planted by Capability Brown in the 18th c.

Motoring Tours

Here are six suggested motoring tours from Bath: allow the best part of a day for each. Names in brackets indicate diversions from main route.

Tour 1 *Longleat and Warminster*
A36 – Bathampton – Claverton – Limpley Stoke – (Hinton Priory) – (A366, Farleigh Castle) – (A366, Norton St Philip) – (Rode Tropical Bird Gardens) – Beckington – A361 to Frome – A362 – (Longleat) – Warminster – A350 to Westbury – B3098 – (Westbury White Horse, Bratton Castle) – Edington – minor road to Steeple Ashton and A350 – A361 to Trowbridge – A363 to Bradford-on-Avon – Bath

Tour 2 *Wells, Cheddar and the Mendips*
A4 W – A39 – Chewton Mendip – Wells – minor road to Wookey Hole Caves – A371 to Cheddar – B3135 – (Priddy) – B3134 – Burrington Combe – A368 – Compton Martin – B3114 – Chew Valley Lake – Chew Stoke – Chew Magna – B3130 – (Stanton Drew) – A37 – A368 – A4 to Bath

Tour 3 *Shepton Mallet*
A367 to Radstock – A362 to Frome – A361 – (Nunney Castle) – (West Cranmore and East Somerset Railway Museum) – Doulting – Shepton Mallet – A37 N – A367 – Oakhill – (Downside Abbey) – Radstock – (B3115 to Priston Mill) – Bath

Tour 4 *Chipping Sodbury and Great Badminton*
A4 E – A46 – (Dyrham Park) – A432 – (Dodington House) – Chipping Sodbury – return to A46 via A432 – (Horton) – B4040 – (Great Badminton) – B4039 – (Castle Combe) – A420 to Chippenham – A4 to Corsham – Box – Bath

Tour 5 *Marlborough*
A4 E – Batheaston – Box – Corsham – Chippenham – (Bowood) – Calne – Cherhill – (Cherhill White Horse) – (Avebury) – Silbury Hill – Overton Hill – (West Kennet Long Barrow) – Marlborough – Marlborough White Horse – A345 S – minor road on Kennet & Avon Canal route to Alton Barnes and on to A361 – Devizes – A365 – Melksham – A350 N – Lacock – minor road to Corsham and A4 – Bath

Tour 6 *Stonehenge*
A36 – Warminster – (Battlesbury Camp) – Scratchbury Camp – Heytesbury – (Stockton) – A303 – Yarnbury Castle – Stonehenge – A345 – Woodhenge – A342 W – B3098 – Urchfont – Edington – Westbury – A363 – Bradford-on-Avon – Bath

Bath

A Brief History

Gorgon head from Roman Bath

Bath's chronicle begins with its hot springs. Long before the Romans came, and the 18th-century entrepreneurs dreamed of their golden city, the springs were bubbling up from the ground. According to legend their curative powers were discovered by Bladud, son of the ancient king Hudibras and renowned in literature as the father of Shakespeare's King Lear.

Prince Bladud, so the story runs, suffered from a leprous complaint. Exiled from court, he became a swineherd, looking after pigs with a similar disease. One day, while wandering with his herd beside the River Avon, he was amazed to see his pigs wallow in a nearby steaming swamp and emerge healed. Following suit, he was at once cured of his leprosy. Restored to favour, Bladud eventually became king and established his royal seat at Bath. Building cisterns to retain the thermal waters, he turned the swamp into a spa.

Roman Bath Centuries later, with the arrival of the Romans, the springs achieved their historical renown. Following the Claudian invasion of 43AD, parties of Romans scouted the Mendip hills for lead, as the Phoenicians had done before them. Word soon reached them of the hot springs dedicated to the native Celtic god, Sul. Within 50 years they had built their own bathing establishment on the site, naming it Aquae Sulis – 'Sul's Springs'. The new township, built at the junction of the Fosse Way with the London, Wales and Dorset roads, soon became a major centre of Roman road communications.

The focal point of the town,

which included a theatre and forum, was the bath complex (built between 68-350 AD) with a splendid temple dedicated to Sul-Minerva, the combined Celtic and Roman deities. In its heyday Aquae Sulis was famed far and wide; its baths, like those at Trier and Wiesbaden, drew Roman visitors not only from Britain but also from north-east Europe and beyond. For wounded and rheumaticky Roman soldiers, the warm waters and recreative club atmosphere must have come as a welcome relief after the rigours of cold northern climes.

After three and a half centuries of uneasy rule the Romans left Britain. Aquae Sulis was one of the cities which fell to invading Saxon forces in the 6th century. Within a short time memories of the Roman occupation had largely faded, and an 8th-century poet was to refer to the baths simply as 'the work of giants'. The neglected buildings fell into ruin and were soon submerged by the swamp.

Benefactor bishops In the 6th century a new form of worship was introduced beside the hot springs. St David established a community of Celtic monks, and a hundred years later Abbess Bertana was granted land for a nunnery 'near the City of Hat Bathu'. A church was established and in 973 AD Edgar was crowned first King of all England at Bath, bringing with him an order of Benedictine monks who were to rule the city for over 500 years.

Civil strife followed the death of William the Conqueror, during the course of which Bath was virtually destroyed. But the city's fortunes recovered when John de Villula of Tours, court physician and from 1088 Bishop of Somersetshire, bought Bath for a token sum and, deciding that the city would make a better seat than Wells, built himself a palace and a vast new abbey church. He also constructed the King's Bath for the use of his royal guests. By this time sick people were making their way to Bath from every part of the country to bathe in the healing waters; so too were their healthier counterparts, 'to see these wonderful burstings out of warm water and to bathe in them', as the *Gesta Stephani* (1138) put it. The monastic St John's Hospital, founded *c*. 1180 as a city charity for the treatment of sick pilgrims, still flourishes today.

It was at about this time that a fierce dispute broke out between the Bath ecclesiastics and the Canons of Wells as to who should elect the bishop; the power struggle raged for a while before it was decided that the bishop should be jointly elected as Bishop of Bath *and* Wells, with his seat at Wells.

Mecca for the poor During the early Middle Ages Bath flourished under monastic rule. Wool was the area's main industry and weaving, introduced in the 14th century, made the city famous (Chaucer's Wife of Bath in his *Canterbury Tales* was so skilled, she 'passed them of Ypres and of Ghent'). But the Black Death of 1349 decimated the monastic population and lowered the morale of those who remained – so much so that a century and a half later Bishop Oliver King felt steps must be taken to restore discipline and rebuild the by then dilapidated church. He worked hard at what he

believed to be his divinely appointed task. However, events overtook him. In 1539 the monastery was officially dissolved and its buildings sold. The Abbey, partially rebuilt and awaiting a new roof, was bought by Edmund Colthurst, MP for Bath; several years later he presented it, together with the churchyard, to the citizens of Bath. When she saw the state of the church building in 1574, Queen Elizabeth I was moved to sponsor a fund for its restoration.

Gradually, as Bath's weaving industry declined, the city became reliant solely upon its attractions as a spa and watering-place. By 1554 the Cross Bath, Hot Bath and King's Bath were under the control of the city authorities, together with a newly-built Lepers' Bath and Horse Bath. The baths became a mecca for the sick poor; so many beggars were now crowding the streets that the country's new vagrancy laws referred to Bath by name. But times were changing. While the baths were traditionally regarded as the prerogative of the poor, influential doctors began to extol the virtues of the thermal waters to their richer patients. Wealthy invalids were soon to be seen in the city, and as their numbers grew, so did those of the fraudulent 'quack' doctors' following in their wake.

Royal favour In 1576 a new bath was opened. This was named the Queens's Bath in 1613 in honour of Anne of Denmark, consort of James I. In 1692 another Anne (Princess, later Queen Anne) also visited Bath. It was her subsequent patronage that set the seal on Bath as a fashionable resort, and she was followed by a succession of royalty, including Charles II, his Queen (and later his mistresses), and James II and his Queen.

Court circles were quick to follow the royal precept. But, as they soon found out, the city was ill-equipped to cater to their needs. The inns were overcrowded, the streets unpaved and unlit, infested with pickpockets, beggars and sedan-chair bullies. Nothing existed in the way of entertainment, apart from gambling (run mainly by card-sharpers) and viewing the nude mixed bathing (a practice considered a scandal by some, and a delight by others such as the diarist Samuel Pepys). This, then, was the seedy state of the city at the turn of the 18th century.

'Beau' Nash Bath's subsequent transformation during the reigns of the four Georges can be attributed to the vision and effort of three self-made men: Richard Nash, Ralph Allen and John Wood. The twenty-year-old Welshman Richard 'Beau' Nash arrived in Bath in 1705 with empty pockets and high ambition. His native gambling skill combined with his social graces soon won him a place in high society, and after only a short time he found himself appointed Master of Ceremonies and *ex officio* King of Bath. Although the position of MC held little civic power, Nash proved himself to be a formidable reformer and organiser. Almost at once he set about raising funds to improve the city's amenities – cleaning up, paving and lighting the streets, controlling the recalcitrant sedan chairmen by issuing licences, and rebuilding the down-at-heel Gravel Walks. In 1706 he amassed a fund

The Pump Room, Bath

to build the first Pump Room on the site where the present building stands, and with typical flair added six musicians to enhance the social appeal of the Room. He followed up this success in 1708 by instigating the building of the first Assembly House between Terrace Walk and the river; named after Thomas Harrison, the Rooms included a card-room and tea-room. A ballroom was added in 1720 and immediately the Rooms, with an added attraction in the form of Assembly Room Concerts, became the social hub of Bath.

Perhaps Nash's most important innovation as *arbiter elegantiae* was to publish a code of manners for visitors. With different levels of polite society mixing freely in the city – a social phenomenon unknown elsewhere in the country – the nobility tended to behave very condescendingly, while the country gentry and rich merchants making up the remainder of Bath society were, for their part, often ignorant of the niceties of behaviour in high society. Nash's rules forbade the wearing of informal and outdoor dress such as aprons or riding boots; duelling was banned and gambling brought under some degree of control. Since Bath was primarily a health resort it was decreed that balls were to end promptly on the stroke of eleven. Nash's most radical move was to stipulate that all social life should be communal: he countenanced neither private dinner parties nor

Comforts of Bath *(Thomas Rowlandson)*

exclusive balls within the city. Curiously enough, most people followed his pronouncements without a murmur of protest; what is more, his code of conduct spread throughout the country, becoming as established a part of 18th-century 'taste' as the classical buildings and landscaped gardens.

Ralph Allen Bath's second well-known entrepreneur, Ralph Allen, became the city's deputy postmaster in 1712, at the age of 18, under the influence of General Wade (later to be MP for Bath). Rising quickly to the position of chief postmaster, Allen married Wade's natural daughter and, with his father-in-law's financial backing, set about reorganising the postal service, making a fortune for himself in the process. He then decided to cash in on the growing vogue for classical building and bought stone quarries on Combe Down outside Bath. The ingenious tramway and pulley system he devised to transport his stone down to the river has become a legend in the early history of the railway. As for his stone-quarries – their legacy can be seen in the fine pale gold buildings which are the city's most obvious attraction.

Rising to be Mayor of Bath in 1742, Allen went on to spend some of his wealth in building Prior Park, a Palladian mansion designed to show off the high quality of his stone. Here, during the next twenty years, he entertained the most famous men of his time. Alexander Pope, Henry Fielding, and his sister Sarah, William Hoare, Thomas Gainsborough, James Quin, Samuel Richardson and David Garrick were among the guests who graced his table. Fielding, who dedicated *Tom Jones* to Allen and partly modelled Squire Allworthy on him, referred to his 'goodness superior to all men' and to his great acts of charity.

John Wood It was the third of the trio, John Wood the Elder, who created a lasting memorial to the city's achievement – the city itself. At the age of 20 he formulated a plan to transform Bath into a second Rome, with its own Royal Forum, Grand Circus and Imperial Gymnasium. Following the lead of Colen Campbell and Lord Burlington he enthusiastically embraced the ideals of classical architecture detailed by Andrea Palladio, a 16th-century Italian architect whose book, *Quattro Libri dell' Architettura*, was changing the face of 18th-century design. The City Corporation rejected out of hand most of Wood's grandiose schemes so he was forced to undertake private commissions. Having rebuilt St John's Hospital and Chapel Court for the Duke of Chandos in 1727, he went on to design new Assembly Rooms on Terrace Walk opposite Harrison's Rooms; these were known first as Lindsey's, then as Wiltshire's Rooms.

Wood was now able to assume the role of entrepreneur – acquiring leases on a chosen plot of land and inviting local builders to construct, behind a façade of his own design, houses and lodgings to suit the individual needs of their clients. In this way he built his first masterpiece, Queen Square, in 1729; this was followed by Prior Park. In 1738, under the auspices of Beau Nash, Ralph Allen and Dr William Oliver (the inventor of the Bath Oliver biscuit), funds were raised to enable Wood to build the Royal Mineral Water Hospital catering for Bath's visiting sick.

By now the need for more lodgings became pressing, and 1739 saw Wood designing North Parade, then South Parade fronting onto the site of what he hoped would become the Royal Forum (this plan never came to fruition). In 1754 he planned his most original scheme, for The Circus, but he died soon after; it was his son John Wood the Younger who actually carried out his father's plan. Today, walking from Wood Street through Queen Square, up Gay Street and into The Circus, the visitor is surrounded by the genius of John Wood the Elder.

Growth of a city Wood died in 1754, Nash in 1761, and Allen in 1764. All three saw Bath's social peak which, strangely enough, did not coincide with the city's architectural heyday during the second half of the century; for as Bath grew more popular, royalty and the aristocracy who made up the fashion-leaders or 'ton' moved to lesser-known resorts such as Brighton.

Between 1705 and 1800 Bath's population increased from 2000 to 34,000. As a result speculators, architects and builders jostled for an opportunity to join the building boom. To begin with, the city spread northwards to what is now Upper Bath; between 1767 and 1774 John Wood the Younger built the Royal Crescent, starting work in 1769 on the New or Upper Assembly Rooms. Thomas Baldwin,

who was appointed City Surveyor in 1775, designed the Guildhall, followed by Somersetshire Buildings and the Octagon, and in 1775 he rebuilt the Hot Bath. Meanwhile, Sir William Pulteney started to develop his Bathwick estate on the east side of the river. He commissioned Robert Adam to build Pulteney Bridge; following Sir William's death Baldwin took over Adam's plan for the rest of the estate, incorporating Adam's ideas into his own scheme, which included the building of Argyle Street, Henrietta Street and Great Pulteney Street. Unfortunately, the financial repercussions of the French Revolution ruined Baldwin; his designs for Sydney Gardens and Sydney Hotel eventually had to be completed by C. Harcourt-Masters in 1796. During the time he was working on the Bathwick estate Baldwin also rebuilt the Cross Baths and the entire baths area and redesigned the Pump Room (which was ultimately re-built by John Palmer in the period 1789-99).

During the 1790s the city went on expanding. John Palmer built Lansdown Crescent and St James's Square; John Eveleigh built Somerset Place, Camden Crescent and started work on the Grosvenor Hotel (now Grosvenor Place), which was to be the first step in his abortive scheme to develop a riverside pleasure ground off the London Road. Building continued on into the Regency period; John Pinch I designed the city's last great terrace, Sion Hill Place, between 1818 and 1820. By then the need for new buildings had declined. People no longer admired the Palladian style; Gothic Revival had become all the rage. Polite society still came to Bath, but as Jane Austen wrote in *Northanger Abbey*, there was 'not a genteel face to be seen' in the Pump Room on Sundays. Nor was there a Beau Nash to hold society together; instead, the city was fast being taken over by social climbers, *nouveaux riches* and fortune-hunters.

Preserving the past, preparing a future With the advent of Brunel's Great Western Railway and the subsequent decline of the Kennet & Avon Canal, Bath's identity changed once again. Soon the GWR was joined by the Midland, which terminated at Green Park Station, and by the Somerset & Dorset mining railway. As industry took a hold, factories grew up along the river and beside the Bristol Road.

In 1878 the City Engineer discovered the Roman Great Bath while investigating a leak in the King's Bath. The ensuing excavations created a new wave of interest and visitors once again started arriving in Bath – which by now had become a haven for retired professional people.

During the Second World War Bath received a new injection of residents, this time in the form of the Ministry of Defence Navy Department. The War left its mark on the city; during the 1942 'Baedeker' raids the Luftwaffe destroyed parts of the Royal Crescent and the Circus, Lansdown Place East and West, the south side of Queen Square, gutted the Assembly Rooms and completely wiped out the area around Avon Street. Ironically, so-called 'rebuilding' schemes of the late 1950s and 1960s resulted in equally wanton destruction of Georgian buildings. During this period most of 'artisan' Bath was bulldozed out of existence to make way for ugly and inappropriate developments such as Snow Hill. This had some impact on the visual integrity of the city, so dependent on the relationship between the Georgian architecture and the surrounding landscape. Fortunately, since that time, the penalties imposed for destroying a listed building without ministerial sanction have helped protect other parts of the city at risk; while the continual watchdog work of the Bath Preservation Trust has led to a growing public awareness of Bath's heritage and to the cleaning and restoration of its Georgian buildings, both great and small.

Bath's severe traffic problem poses another threat to the 18th-century city and still remains to be solved; a proposal for a motorway running near the city centre was vetoed a few years ago, but so far no alternative scheme has proved feasible. Meanwhile, Bath continues to excite public interest with sites of historical importance. Archeologists are currently engaged in the excavation and partial reconstruction of the precint of the Roman Temple of Sulis Minerva, long buried under the Pump Room. Most challenging is the plan to build a new spa complex with sophisticated treatment rooms and hotels. This will mean that in the not too distant future, visitors will see Roman and 20th-century baths lying within a few hundred yards of each other – spanning 2000 years of this great city's history.

The City of Bath

Population 84,670

Tourist Information Abbey
Churchyard. Tel Bath (0225) 62831.
Jun-mid Sep, daily 10-6; mid-Sep-
May, daily 10-5

Parking *Car Parks* Avon Street; Broad
Street; Charlotte Street; Manvers
Street; *Street Parking* Green Park;
Ham Gardens; Kingsmead; Walcot
Street; Sawclose

Post Office New Bond Street

Shopping Milsom Street; Union
Street; Stall Street; Southgate;
Covered Market (entrance High
Street, Grand Parade);
Northumberland Place; Corridor;
Union Passage; Broad Street. (Early
closing Thur)

Market Days Wed: Antique market,
Guinea Lane; Sat: Bric-a-brac market
in the cattle market, Walcot Street

Theatre Theatre Royal, Sawclose

Events West of England Antiques Fair
(May); Bath Festival (May/June);
Somerset County Cricket Festival,
Bath Round Table Carnival (June);
Floral Festival (July); Book Week
(Nov)

Sport & Recreation see p. 16

Places of Interest
*Descriptions of these places are given in
the Walks, which follow. See Index for
page references*

Churches

Abbey Church of St Peter and St Paul
Abbey Churchyard

St John Catholic Church South
Parade

St Mary Bathwick

St Michael Broad Street

St Stephen Lansdown Road

St Swithin's Church Paragon

Historic Buildings

**Assembly Rooms and Costume
Museum** Bennett Street and Alfred
Street
Summer: Mon-Sat 9.30-6; Sun 10-6
Winter: Mon-Sat 10-5; Sun 11-5

Green Park Station corner of James
Street West
Built 1869-70 as Bath terminus of the
Midland Railway and from 1874 a
station on the Somerset and Dorset
line. Fine classical façade, train shed
supported on iron girders.

Guildhall High Street
Mon-Fri 9-4.30

No 1 Royal Crescent
Mar-Oct, Tue-Sat 11-5; Sun 2-5

Pump Room Abbey Churchyard
Summer: Apr-Oct, daily, 9-6; Jul-
Aug, daily, 9-7
Winter: Nov-Mar, Mon-Sat 9-5; Sun
11-5

Sally Lunn's House North Parade
Passage
Normal shopping hours

Parks and Gardens

Alexandra Park Beechen Cliff

Henrietta Park Henrietta Street

Parade Gardens Grand Parade

**Royal Victoria Park and Botanic
Gardens** Queens Parade

Sydney Gardens Sydney Place

Castles, Ruins and Ancient Sites

Roman Baths and Temple Precinct
Abbey Churchyard
See *Pump Room*

Eastgate Orange Grove, Grand Parade

Upper Borough Walls

Sally Lunn's House

Museums and Galleries

Bath Carriage Museum Circus Mews
Summer: Mon-Sat 9.30-6; Sun 10-6
Winter: Mon-Sat 10-5; Sun 11-5

Bath Postal Museum 51 Great
Pulteney Street
Mon-Tue, Thur-Sat 11-5; Sun 2-5

Burrows Toy Museum York Street
Daily 10-5.30

Camden Works Museum Julian Road
Easter-Sep, daily 2-5; Oct-Easter,
daily except Fri 2-5

Geology Museum 18 Queen Square
Mon-Fri 10-6; Sat 10-5. Closed Sun,
Bank Hol

Herschel House and Museum
19 New King Street
Home of Sir William Herschel from
which he discovered the planet Uranus
in 1781. 18th-c. furniture, displays of
astronomy and music.
Mar-Oct, Wed & Sat 2-5

Holburne of Menstrie Museum
Great Pulteney Street
Tue-Sat 11-5; Sun 2.30-6. Closed Dec &
Jan

Museum of Bookbinding
Manvers Street
Extension of the firm of George
Bayntun, booksellers and binders.
Exhibition showing the history of
bookbinding.
Weekdays, business hours

Museum of Costume see *Assembly
Rooms*

Rail Lines Avon Street opposite car
park
Robert Bunyar's collection of railway
relics and curios, with books and
secondhand model railway items.
Tue-Sat 10.30-12.45 & 2-4

Roman Baths Museum see *Pump
Room*

Royal Photographic Society Centre
Milsom Street
Mon-Sat 10-4.45; Sun during summer
hol 11-4

Victoria Art Gallery
Mon-Fri 10-6; Sat 10-5. Closed Sun
and Bank Hol

Homes of the Famous

The following list includes a few of the illustrious men and women who are known to have lodged in Bath during the once-fashionable late summer season, and many more who have taken up residence in the City over the past 200 years.

Allen, Ralph Terrace Walk, Prior Park

André, Major 22 The Circus

Anstey, Christopher 5 Royal Crescent

Austen, Jane 13 Queen Square, 4 Sydney Place

Baldwin, Thomas 6 Great Pulteney Street

Beckford, William 19 & 20 Lansdown Crescent

Burney, Fanny 14 South Parade

Burke, Edmund 11 North Parade

Chesterfield, Earl of 3a & 4 Pierrepont Street

Clarence, Duke of (later William IV) Sydney Place

Clive of India, Lord 14 The Circus

Dickens, Charles 35 St James's Square

Fielding, Henry Widcombe Lodge

Fitzherbert, Mrs 10 Queens Parade

Gainsborough, Thomas 17 The Circus

Goldsmith, Oliver 11 North Parade

Hart, Emma (later Lady Hamilton) Linley House, Pierrepont Place

Herschel, Sir William 19 New King Street

Linley, Elizabeth 11 Royal Crescent

Livingstone, Dr David 13 The Circus

Macaulay, Lord 1 Great Pulteney Street

Prince Louis Napoleon (later Napoleon III) Great Pulteney Street

Nash, Richard 'Beau' Sawclose

Nelson, Admiral Lord 2 Pierrepont Street

Oliver, Dr William 24 Queen Square

Phillip, Admiral Arthur 19 Bennett Street

Pitman, Sir Isaac 17 Royal Crescent

Pitt the Elder, William 15 Johnson Street, 7 & 8 The Circus

Scott, Sir Walter 6 South Parade

Sheridan, Richard Brinsley 9 New King Street

Siddons, Sarah 33 Paragon

Walpole, Horace Hetling House

Wedgwood, Josiah 30 Gay Street

Wesley, John 2 Broad Street

Whistler, James 1 St James Square

Wilberforce, William 36 Great Pulteney Street

Wolfe, General 5 Trim Street

Wood the Elder, John 24 Queen Square

Wood the Younger, John 41 Gay Street

Wordsworth, William 9 North Parade

Short excursions from Bath

The places listed below are within a short distance by bus or car from the city centre and worth a visit (for information, see Gazetteer entries).

Batheaston
Bathford
Bathampton
Beckford's Tower and Museum
Claverton and American Museum
Little Solsbury Hill
Prior Park
Sham Castle
Widcombe

Bath Walks

Free Guided Tours to the city are offered during the summer season (Jun-Sep). These are walking tours of about 2hrs duration. The times of the tours, which start from the Abbey Churchyard, may be obtained from the Tourist Information Office.

Ghost Walk Starting outside *The Garrick Head* beside the Theatre Royal in Sawclose. Phenomena explored range from poltergeists in the Nash Bar to the groans from the burial ground in Upper Borough Walls. Not for the faint-hearted. Walks take place May-Oct, Mon-Fri & Nov-Apr, Fri only 8pm. For details, Tel (0225) 310134

Detail W front, Bath Abbey

Walk 1 Lower Bath
Starting point: **Abbey Churchyard**

This small paved square, a pleasant place for sitting or strolling, is Bath's historic centre, for here are the two monuments to its unique heritage: the baths of Aquae Sulis and the great church whose W front dominates the square.

Bath Abbey has a history of over 1200 years, going back to the Saxon Abbey that was built in the vicinity of this site *c.* 781. The Christian tradition had been established here by St David of Wales, who is credited with the rediscovery of the hot springs and the settlement of a community of Celtic monks in the area in the mid-6th c. AD. In the next century the community was visited by St Augustine, on one of his missionary journeys, and subsequently St Aldhelm, the founder of Malmesbury Abbey, brought the monastery under his wing with many benefactions. The eventual patronage of the kings of Mercia culminated in the creation of a royal borough and the foundation of the

first Abbey. The greatest event in the Abbey's history, the coronation of Edgar, the first king of a united England, took place in 973.

The Saxon Abbey, destroyed in a conflict between the barons and King William Rufus, was replaced in 1107 by a splendid Norman cathedral. This was the work of John de Villula, Bishop of Bath, who for a token sum had purchased the war-ravaged city from the king. The new building, 354ft long and 72ft wide, was considerably larger than the present Abbey.

By the end of the 15th c. the cathedral had become ruinous and Bishop Oliver King undertook the construction of the present Abbey, which now stands as the last great church of the Perpendicular period. The masons were Robert and William Vertue, who also worked on two famous national monuments: the Chapel of Henry VII at Westminster Abbey and the Royal Chapel of St George in Windsor Castle. A common feature of the three buildings is the superb fan vaulting.

The *W front* is Bishop King's personal inspiration. The faces of the turrets are decorated with ladders of angels ascending and descending: at the sides stand the Twelve Apostles, while on either side of the W doorway are the figures of St Peter and St Paul. The Dissolution interrupted the rebuilding work, but in 1572 the Abbey and its churchyard were presented to the citizens of Bath. Two years later while visiting the city, Queen Elizabeth I was so distressed by the dilapidated state of the Abbey that she ordered collections for the restoration of the building. The splendid oak *W door* (1617) carved with the arms of Bishop Montague, who carried out subsequent restoration work, dates from this period. Since then, the Abbey has seen many changes. Today's building is the result of later generations trying to recreate what they believed early Tudor builders would have constructed had circumstances not intervened. G.P. Manners added the pinnacles and hollow flying buttresses during the 1820s.

The entrance is to the left of the W door. The Abbey has been called the 'Lantern of the West' because of its exceptionally large clerestory windows above the nave and choir. Its other remarkable feature is the enormous number of memorials (614) – more than any other English church apart from Westminster Abbey. The elegant fan vaulting is of two periods: that of the chancel, aisles and transepts 16th c. and that of the nave the 1860s restoration of Sir George Gilbert Scott, based on the Vertues' designs. Scott also designed the chandeliers.

Moving up the *N aisle*, the largest monument in the church belongs to James Montague, Bishop of Bath and Wells 1608-16, who contributed greatly to the restoration of the church. On the wall opposite is a memorial to Sir Isaac Pitman (d. 1897). The *N transept* contains a fine organ, a rebuilding (1972) of an 18th-c. Abraham Jordan original (the black oak figure of King David by the stairway belonged to the original organ). The wrought-iron grille was once an altar rail, given in 1725.

The narrow rectangular *crossing* is the result of the present Abbey being built on the nave of its Norman predecessor: the piers of the crossings are in the position of the original Norman nave piers. The transepts are correspondingly narrow, and the central tower rectangular rather than square. A stone slab by the lectern commemorates the visit of the Queen and the Duke of Edinburgh to give thanks for 1000 years of the English monarchy.

At the W end of the *N chancel aisle* is a memorial to Admiral Arthur Phillip (d. 1814), founder of Australia's first British settlement. At the E end is the Edgar window, depicting King Edgar's coronation in the Abbey in 973 by the two Archbishops: the ceremony used at Bath forms the basis of the coronation ceremony performed today. Nearby stands an early 18th-c. font with an octagonal wooden cover: on the wall a tablet to James Quin the 18th-c. comic actor, with an epitaph composed by his friend and fellow actor David Garrick.

Bath Abbey

The *sanctuary* is now entered, and here the beautiful *E window* can be studied. Blown out by a landmine in 1942, it was restored by M.C. Farrar Bell: the 817sq ft of glass contain 56 scenes from the life of Christ. On the S side is the finely carved *Prior Birde Chantry* (1515). The chapel next door at the E end of the S aisle contains the only surviving part of the Norman cathedral visible above ground: a round arch which originally gave access from the nave aisle to the transept of the 12th-c. church. It now encloses a memorial window to Bishop John de Villula. Outside the chapel is an interesting portable wooden font (18th c.).

In the *S transept* is the alabaster tomb of Jane Waller (d. 1633), wife of Sir William Waller, a Parliamentary general defeated at the Battle of Lansdown in 1643. Further on in the *S aisle* a plain tablet commemorates Bath's famous Master of Ceremonies, Richard 'Beau' Nash (d. 1761).

Emerging from the Abbey, the fine Georgian house on the right (1720) is now occupied by the National Trust. On the opposite side of the square further down is the entrance to the Pump Room and Roman Baths (The Abbey Churchyard entrance is closed during the winter months: the alternative entrance is in Stall Street).

The Great Bath

The **Pump Room** was designed by Thomas Baldwin and completed by John Palmer, 1789-92, replacing an earlier building of 1706, the first on the site. The N front has Ionic columns and a Greek inscription meaning 'Water is Best'. The interior provides an elegant starting point for a tour of the baths, with its Corinthian columns, curved recesses and musicians' gallery. Beau Nash's statue occupies the E alcove; below it is the clock given to the city by its maker Thomas Tompion in 1709. The W alcove has a musician's gallery. In the spa's heyday the Pump Room was its social centre: visitors can still sample the waters whilst a trio plays.

Beyond lie the Roman Baths and Temple Precinct of Aquae Sulis. The continuing excavations here are arousing great interest. The **Roman Baths** (68-350AD) were part of a great bathing, religious and leisure complex which included a theatre and a temple dedicated to Sulis Minerva, a compound of the Roman goddess of healing, Minerva, and the ancient Celtic god Sul. After the departure of the Romans the elaborate bath they had constructed around the warm springs gradually disappeared. It was not until 1727, some time after the spa had been re-activated, that workmen digging a sewer came across a gilded bronze head of Minerva. Another 150 years was to pass before the discovery of the Great Bath (1878).

A descent is made through the various levels built up over the centuries to the Roman Baths **Museum**. This houses the treasures uncovered during the past 200 years. Pride of place goes to the bronze head of Minerva and to a remarkable barbaric stone head depicting a moustachioed and winged Celtic god – once the centrepiece of the temple pediment. Other exhibits include fragments from the *Façade of the Four Seasons* and the *Luna Pediment*, altar corner blocks and votive offerings. Beneath the Pump Room, in the recently excavated **Temple Precinct**, can be seen the altar itself and the doorway and steps leading to the sacred spring.

The tour of the baths themselves commences with the *Great Bath*, the central bath of the complex. This is fed by underground springs at the rate of 250,000 gallons a day at a constant temperature of 48° C. It is still lined with the original Roman lead sheeting, and some of the lead pipes supplying the water to the different baths of the complex are still in position. The recesses on either side, originally used for sitting out, now display architectural details.

The *East Baths* were a suite of heated rooms, possibly reserved for female bathers. To the W of the Great Bath is the *Circular Bath*, a cold plunge bath; from here, climbing a few steps, there is a view through a Roman window of the *King's Bath*, lying above the Roman reservoir and hot spring. The .last section, the *West Baths*, consists of an oval swimming bath, a well-preserved hypocaust and a suite of hot rooms. Exit is through a souvenir shop.

Here, at the Stall Street exit, the façade of the Baths links architecturally with the colonnades of Bath Street opposite. Walking to the far end of Bath Street, to the left stands the **Hot Bath** or **Old Royal Bath**, while ahead is the **Cross Bath**, dating from medieval times. Plans are afoot to construct a new international spa resort and hotels in which the Hot Bath will be developed as a treatment centre. Tucked behind the Cross Bath is one of the city's oldest backwaters, **Chapel Court**, and within it is the *Hospital of St John*, founded by Bishop Reginald of Bath *c.* 1180, and rebuilt by John Wood I in 1727. Still active, it is one of the most ancient charities. *Hetling House*, next door, now the Abbey Church House, is a 16th-c. town house built for Sir Walter Hungerford of Farleigh Castle.

Now turn left into Hot Bath Street, left again into Beau Street, right into Stall Street and left into Abbey Gate Street, continuing along and through the arch. *Abbey Green* with its spreading plane tree is lined with a fascinating variety of 17th, 18th and 19th-c. buildings; it is believed to have been the medieval monks' bowling green. Take the top left exit into York Street and on the left is **Burrows Toy Museum**. The Museum's collection of playthings ranges from dolls and their houses to constructional toys. Adults particularly will enjoy the 1920s and 1930s promotional toys: Shirley Temple dolls, Ovaltineys' comics – even a Neville Chamberlain doll. William Harbutt, the inventor of plasticine, is commemorated in a large plasticine model. Emerging from the Museum, turn right along York Street to what is now the *Friends' Meeting House*, built as the Freemasons' Hall in 1819 by

William Wilkins, architect of London's National Gallery.

Backtrack a few yards and turn left into Church Street, then left again into North Parade Passage. Here stands the oldest house in Bath, **Sally Lunn's House** (1482), formerly part of a house belonging to the Dukes of Kingston. Sally Lunn took over the tenancy in 1680, and such was her reputation as a pastrycook, her coffee rooms soon became the most fashionable in the city. After a period of ownership by Ralph Allen (from 1725) it reverted to being a coffee house – and still does a roaring trade in its original-recipe muffins known as 'Sally Lunns'. Downstairs in the basement the original ovens still survive, while opening off the old kitchen is an ancient grotto with stalagmites and stalactites.

Turning left into Terrace Walk, between Nos 1 and 2 can be glimpsed the façade of *Ralph Allen's Town House* (1727), which served as Allen's first post office. Entrance to the courtyard is between an antique shop and the Friends' Meeting House in York Street. Near the distant skyline to the E is the castellated folly Sham Castle, an eye-catcher which Allen built to enjoy from his window.

Entering North Parade, turn right at the traffic lights into Pierrepont Street, right again into Pierrepont Place and left into Orchard Street. The *Masonic Hall* (Thomas Jelly, 1750) was formerly the Theatre Royal, where the tragic actress Sarah Siddons first made her name. This theatre, although extremely popular, was ultimately found to be too small and replaced by the new Theatre Royal in Beaufort Square in 1805 (see below). Turn left into Henry Street, cross Pierrepont Street and continue on into South Parade. The wide pavement is all that was ever built of John Wood I's scheme for a Royal Forum. *St John's Catholic Church* (1861-3) on the right is a distinctive, stone-faced Gothic building with a spire based on Lincolnshire models; its architect, Charles Hanson, also designed Clifton College in Bristol.

Turn left into Duke Street and left again into North Parade (both by John Wood I, 1740-48). At the traffic lights cross North Parade and continue straight on with the *Parade Gardens* below on the right. An orchestra or brass band plays in the formal gardens during the summer season, and each year a new flower sculpture is created to enhance the flower walks. To the left is the *Orange Grove*, now marked by a roundabout and an obelisk. Originally a squalid area known as the Gravel Walks, the grove was greatly improved by Beau Nash, who organised the planting of trees and set the obelisk to commemorate a visit made by William, Prince of Orange in 1734.

Cross the road to the *Empire Hotel* (Charles Edward Davis, 1899) opposite. Nothing could be more of a contrast to Bath's 18th-c. elegance than this neo-Jacobean block. The hotel's five storeys are topped by a mock cottage, a Loire-style gable and a tower. The Ministry of Defence (Navy) has occupied the building since the Second World War.

A yard to the left of the building can be followed round to Grand Parade. On the right, below ground level, can be seen **Eastgate**, Bath's only surviving medieval gateway.

Cross to the river side of Grand Parade, and pause to see why Bath has so often been compared with Florence. Below, the River Avon flows through a delightful curved weir, built in the 1970s. Spanning the river is the three-arched **Pulteney Bridge**. There is no other bridge like it in England; the only comparable bridge built end to end with small shops is Florence's Ponte Vecchio. Sir William Pulteney, owner of the Bathwick estate on the far side of the river, commissioned Robert Adam, then the country's leading architect, to build it. The bridge, completed in 1774, is Adam's only work in Bath.

Across Pulteney Bridge, Argyle Street leads into Laura Place, with a central fountain. The Place, together with its surrounding streets, are the work of Thomas Baldwin and were completed in the 1790s. Henrietta

Pulteney Bridge

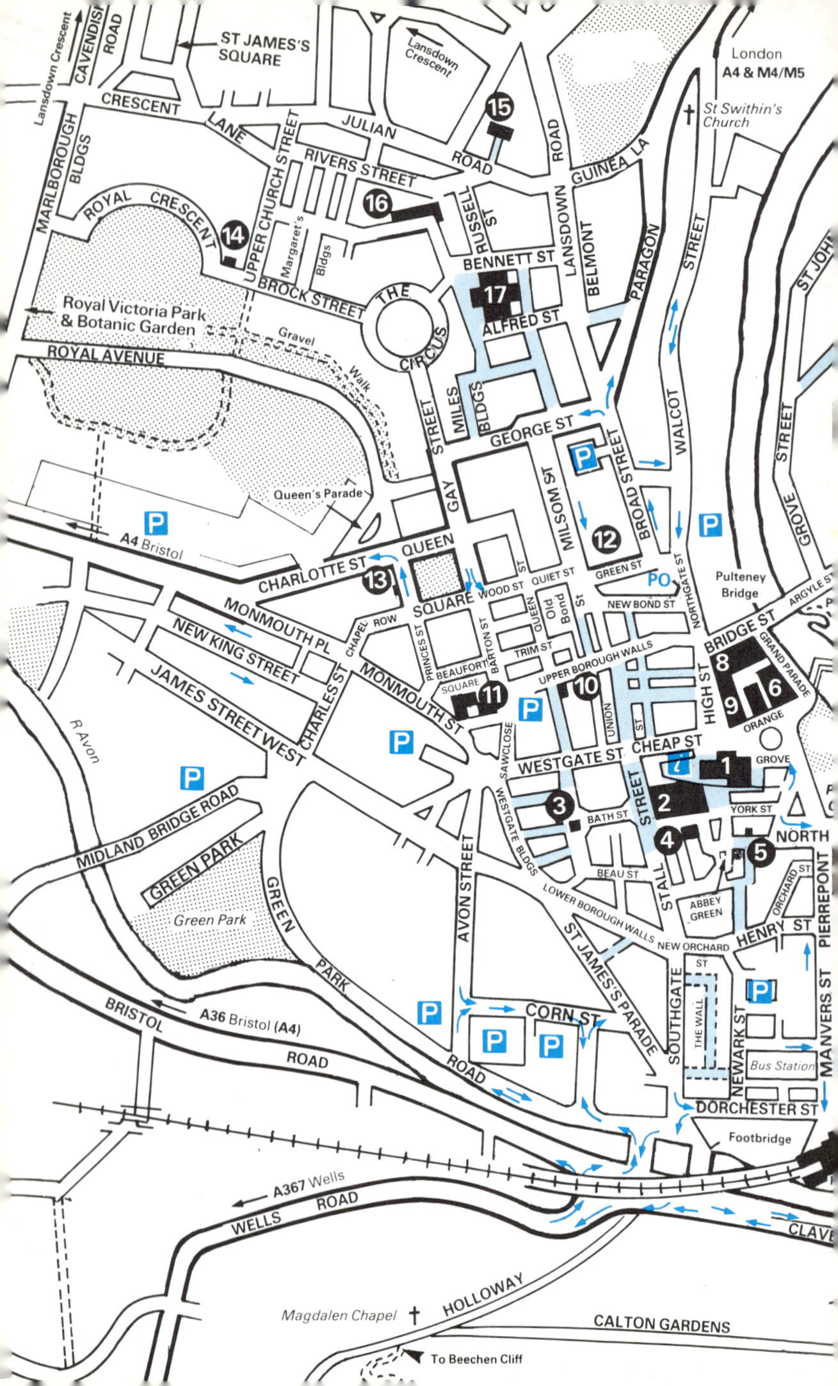

Lansdown Crescent
CAVENDISH ROAD
ST JAMES'S SQUARE
CRESCENT
MARLBOROUGH BLDGS
LANE
JULIAN
RIVERS STREET
Lansdown Crescent
ROAD
15
ROYAL CRESCENT
UPPER CHURCH STREET
16
London A4 & M4/M5
St Swithin's Church
GUINEA LA
RUSSELL ST
14
Margaret's Bldgs
BENNETT ST
LANSDOWN ROAD
BELMONT
PARAGON
STREET
ST JOHN
BROCK STREET
Royal Victoria Park & Botanic Garden
Gravel
THE CIRCUS
17
ALFRED ST
MILES
BLDGS
GEORGE ST
WALCOT
STREET
GROVE STREET
ROYAL AVENUE
Walk
GAY STREET
MILSOM ST
P
BROAD STREET
P
Queen's Parade
QUEEN
12
P
PO
Pulteney Bridge
ARGYLE ST
P
A4 Bristol
CHARLOTTE ST
SQUARE
WOOD ST
QUIET ST
GREEN ST
Northgate St
CHAPEL ROW
13
PRINCES ST
QUEEN ST
Old Bond St
NEW BOND ST
BRIDGE ST
MONMOUTH PL
NEW KING STREET
Bldgs
TRIM ST
Upper Borough Walls
8
GRAND PARADE
BEAUFORT SQUARE
BARTON ST
9
6
CHARLES ST
MONMOUTH ST
11
P
10
ORANGE GROVE
JAMES STREET WEST
SAWCLOSE
UNION ST
HIGH ST
R Avon
WESTGATE ST
CHEAP ST
1
P
P
WESTGATE BLDGS
BATH ST
7
2
P
MIDLAND BRIDGE ROAD
3
STALL STREET
YORK ST
5
NORTH
GREEN PARK
BEAU ST
4
ABBEY GREEN
ORCHARD ST
PIERREPONT
Green Park
GREEN PARK
LOWER BOROUGH WALLS
NEW ORCHARD ST
HENRY ST
MANVERS ST
ST JAMES'S PARADE
SOUTHGATE
THE WALL
P
BRISTOL
A36 Bristol (A4)
CORN ST
Bus Station
NEWARK ST
ROAD
P
P
P
DORCHESTER ST
ROAD
Footbridge
A367 Wells
CLAVE
WELLS ROAD
HOLLOWAY
Magdalen Chapel
CALTON GARDENS
To Beechen Cliff

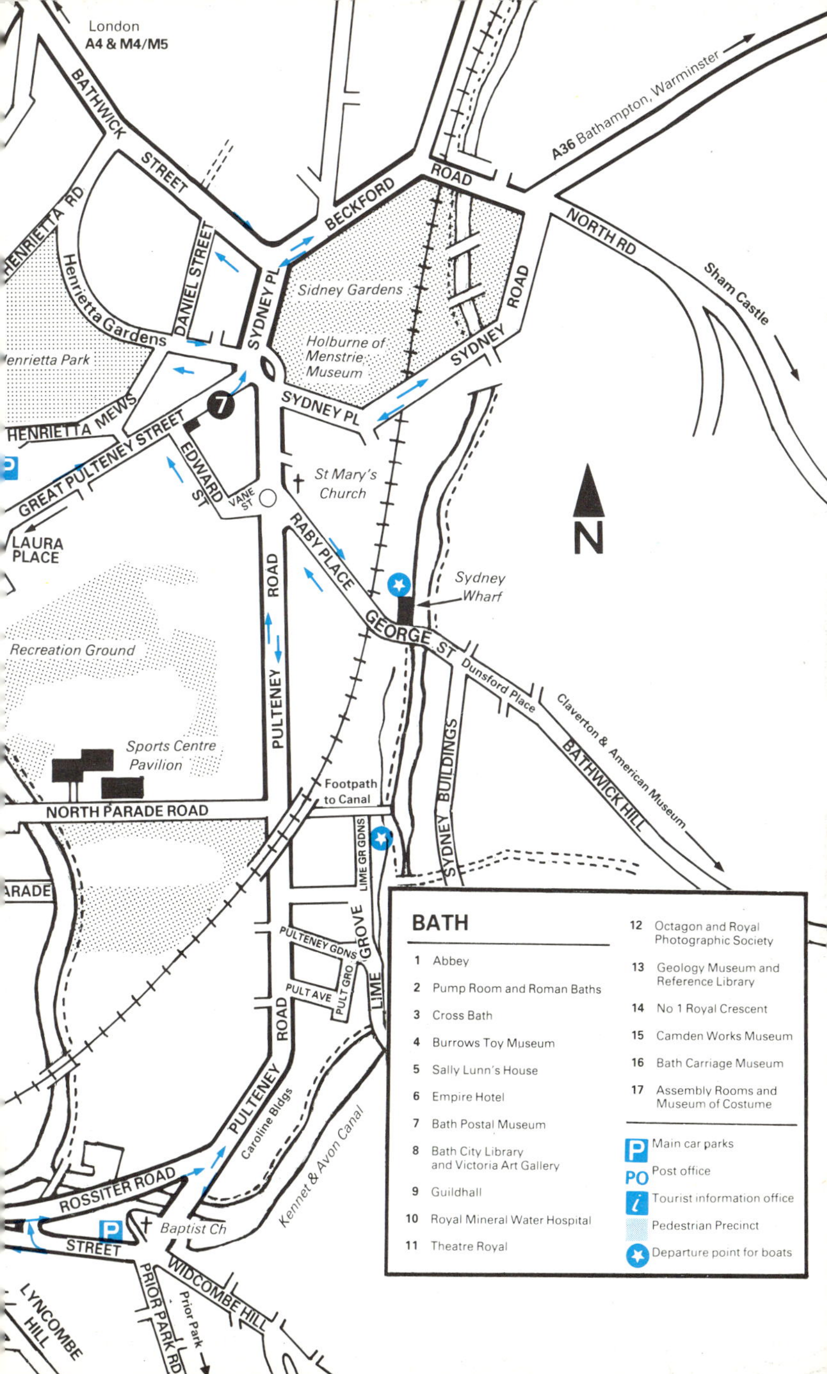

London
A4 & M4/M5
A36 Bathampton, Warminster
BATHWICK STREET
HENRIETTA RD
Henrietta Gardens
DANIEL STREET
SYDNEY PL
BECKFORD ROAD
NORTH RD
Sham Castle
Sidney Gardens
Holburne of Menstrie Museum
SYDNEY ROAD
Henrietta Park
HENRIETTA MEWS
GREAT PULTENEY STREET
EDWARD ST
VANE ST
SYDNEY PL
Henrietta Park
7
P
LAURA PLACE
St Mary's Church
N
Sydney Wharf
Recreation Ground
PULTENEY ROAD
RABY PLACE
GEORGE ST
Dunsford Place
SYDNEY BUILDINGS
Claverton & American Museum
BATHWICK HILL
Sports Centre Pavilion
NORTH PARADE ROAD
Footpath to Canal
LIME GR GDNS
PARADE
PULTENEY ROAD
PULTENEY GDNS
PULT GRO
PULT AVE
LIME GROVE
Caroline Bldgs
Kennet & Avon Canal
ROSSITER ROAD
P
Baptist Ch
STREET
WIDCOMBE HILL
PRIOR PARK RD
Prior Park
LYNCOMBE HILL

BATH
1   Abbey
2   Pump Room and Roman Baths
3   Cross Bath
4   Burrows Toy Museum
5   Sally Lunn's House
6   Empire Hotel
7   Bath Postal Museum
8   Bath City Library and Victoria Art Gallery
9   Guildhall
10 Royal Mineral Water Hospital
11 Theatre Royal
12 Octagon and Royal Photographic Society
13 Geology Museum and Reference Library
14 No 1 Royal Crescent
15 Camden Works Museum
16 Bath Carriage Museum
17 Assembly Rooms and Museum of Costume

P   Main car parks
PO   Post office
i   Tourist information office
     Pedestrian Precinct
     Departure point for boats

Street, to the left, leads off to *Henrietta Park*. Named after Sir William Pulteney's daughter, the park has an unusual sweet-smelling garden designed especially for the blind, with information in Braille. Behind the park lie a number of other pleasant 18th-c. residential streets.

Straight ahead is **Great Pulteney Street** (Thomas Baldwin, *c*. 1788), the finest street in Bath (walk up on the left). It is a spacious, dignified thoroughfare, over 1000ft long and 100ft wide, culminating at the far end in the **Holburne of Menstrie Museum**. The Museum, with its fine pedimented portico and Corinthian columns, was built as the Sydney Hotel (C. Harcourt-Masters, 1796); John Pinch II later adapted the building to house Sir Thomas William Holburne's fine art collection, some of which was inherited, some bought from the William Beckford sale at Lansdown. The collection includes some of the most splendid 17th and 18th-c. silver in Britain, together with Roman glass, cameos, seals and coins, miniatures, ceramics and porcelain. Among the paintings are works by Gainsborough, Guardi, Stubbs, Turner and Zoffany. Sharing the building is the *Crafts Study Centre*, which has changing exhibitions and works by this century's best British craftsmen.

To the S of the museum, along Pulteney Road, is **St Mary's Church**, Bathwick. Built by John Pinch I, 1814-20, this is the most attractive of Bath's Gothic Revival churches, with a tower modelled on Bath Abbey.

Behind the Museum lies *Sydney Gardens* (Thomas Baldwin, 1795) built to rival London's Ranelagh Gardens. The fashionable grottoes, labyrinth and sham castle have long disappeared along with the fireworks and orchestras. All the same, the park is an atmospheric place with, on the one hand, its tree-lined walks and peaceful canal, and on the other, the occasional excitement provided by the high-speed train slowing down to glide along the Great Western Railway line to the station.

Return along Great Pulteney Street. On the left stands the **Bath Postal Museum**, commemorating Bath's contributions to the history of communications. These include John Palmer's introduction of the Royal Mail

Holburne of Menstrie Museum

Coach (known as the 'flying machine') and the young Ralph Allen's successful endeavours to make the postal service efficient and profitable. The Museum possesses the only existing copy of the 1727 contract in which Allen agreed to reorganise the post. Outside, a Victorian wall letter-box is a reminder that the building was once a village sorting office; later, it was the base from which the philatelist Henry Stafford Smith published the first-ever stamp journal.

Cross Pulteney Bridge into Bridge Street. **Bath City Library**, to the left, houses the Abbey Library, founded in 1619; among its treasures is Voragine's *The Golden Legend*, published in 1493 from the press of Caxton's successor, Wynkyn de Worde. The library building is also the home of the **Victoria Art Gallery**, which mounts changing exhibitions – often linked to its own sizeable collection of paintings, porcelain, glass and watches. On permanent view upstairs is the Lichfield Clock, a remarkable musical altar clock made in the shape of a Gothic church, with moving religious figures.

At the junction with High Street, to the left, a doorway leads into the *Covered Market*, founded by Royal Charter in medieval times and still flourishing today. Beside it stands the **Guildhall**, built by Thomas Baldwin in the 1770s to replace Inigo Jones's smaller 17th-c. building; John McKean Brydon added the dome and flanking wings in 1893. The Guildhall's *Banqueting Room* is acknowledged to be the finest interior in Bath, a masterpiece of late 18th-c. decoration. 80ft long, it is perfectly proportioned with delicate moulding throughout, and enhanced by three fine chandeliers.

Crossing High Street and walking N, take a left turn into Upper Borough Walls. On the left, past Union Passage and Union Street, stands what was formerly the **Royal Mineral Water Hospital** (John Wood I, 1736). The hospital was built from public subsciption to provide for the needs of the sick poor. Ralph Allen provided the stone free of charge, Beau Nash was appointed Treasurer, and Dr William Oliver – whose idea the whole project was – became the first president, to be succeeded by General Wade and later by Frederick, Prince of Wales. Traditionally, the hospital never treated Bath citizens – only patients from outside the city. The building has become the Royal National Hospital for Rheumatic Diseases. Further along on the right, a few yards of the city's medieval wall still stand, following the line of the original Roman wall. On the far side of the wall, at a lower level, the concrete-covered area was once the City graveyard.

Upper Borough Walls opens out into Sawclose. Opposite stands *Beau Nash's House* (Thomas Greenway, 1720). St John's Court, of which the house was once part, also included *The Garrick Head* pub, which stands on the far side of the Theatre Royal. Nash's house is now *Popjoy's Restaurant*, named after Nash's mistress Juliana Popjoy, who, after his death in 1761, is said to have spent the rest of her life sleeping in a tree. The **Theatre Royal** next door has had a chequered history. At the time of its opening in 1805 it was acclaimed as the finest theatre in the provinces. Equal in size to the original Covent Garden, the building's N façade facing onto Beaufort Square was designed by John Palmer and executed by George Dance II; inside there were magnificent ceiling panels painted by Casali, bought from William Beckford's collection. During the 1820s, as the attractions of Bath declined, so too did those of its theatre; in 1862 a fire virtually gutted the interior. However, the building was rebuilt inside by C.J. Phipps and the theatre went on to resound to the success of such names as Edmund Kean, Joey Grimaldi, Ellen Terry and Henry Irving. Now restored, the theatre has recently been re-opened in association with the National Theatre.

Walking down Sawclose, turn left into Westgate Street, on into Cheap Street and right through the archway into the Abbey Churchyard.

Walk 2

Starting point: **Milsom Street**

Walk down from the top of the street. On the left, the street is dominated by the *Somersetshire Buildings* (Thomas Baldwin, 1781-88). The Buildings are made up of five houses with pillared and pedimented end-pavilions and a bow-fronted central house, now occupied by the National Westminster Bank.

Further down on the left stands the **Octagon** (Thomas Lightoler, 1767) housing the *Royal Photographic Society Centre*. The Octagon was the most famous of Bath's proprietary chapels (six in all). Built by speculators, they were rented out for substantial pew rents; their owners also made a handsome profit from performing 'Fleet Marriages' – marriage ceremonies for which no licence, banns or parental consent were needed. When first built, the chapel's octagonal shape extended into two semi-circular alcoves; the sanctuary contained an elaborate altarpiece painted by William Hoare. For many years the chapel organist was William Herschel, a former Astronomer Royal who discovered Uranus in 1781. The RPS Centre's Link and Octagon Galleries present changing exhibitions, while up on the Octagon Balcony a permanent exhibition recounts the history of photography from the 1830s to the present day. The display includes the best collection of Leica cameras in the world and three Niépce images.

Cross the road into Quiet Street and continue along Wood Street into **Queen Square** (1728-34). Named after George II's wife Queen Caroline, the square is one of John Wood I's Palladian masterpieces. On the N side the dominating palace front consists of seven large houses grouped to form a symmetrical composition. The central house, a colonnaded and pedimented pavilion, was the home of the architect. The buildings on the E and W side of the square are less imposing. On the S side *The Francis Hotel* is made up of six houses (Nos 6-11) damaged in a 1942 'Baedeker' air raid and later rebuilt.

The Royal Crescent

The Circus

The square's central garden contains an obelisk set up by Richard 'Beau' Nash to honour a visit paid by the Prince and Princess of Wales in 1738. The *Geology Museum* occupies the second floor of the Reference Library on the W side of the square; it contains a number of fossils and other geological specimens collected by the 19th-c. geologist Charles Moore in the Bath and Bristol areas; among them can be seen the 200-million-year-old footprints of an early dinosaur.

Walking round the N side of the square, cross Gay Street (John Wood I and II, 1734-60). The distinctive corner house, **No 41**, was once the home of John Wood II. The three-storeyed bow is decorated with balustrades and pilasters and topped by three urns. Through the window to the right of the Gay Street entrance can be seen a small alcove lined with blue-and-white Delft tiles. This was used as a men's powder room, in the days when wigs were powdered. Continuing up Gay Street, Queen's Parade Place on the left leads to Royal Avenue and the Royal Victoria Park.

Gay Street leads up to one of the city's architectural wonders: The **Circus**. John Wood I planned his new city development with The Circus as its central feature. He died a few months later and it was his son who carried out his design (1754-58). Wood I found his

detract from the dramatic simplicity of the whole. The *Costume and Fashion Research Centre* at No. 4 is an extension of the Museum of Costume, offering research facilities with books, periodicals and photographs to anyone interested in the history of dress.

The W exit of The Circus leads into Brock Street. John Wood II built the street (1765) to link his father's great design with his own scheme. At the end on the right is **No 1 Royal Crescent**. The Bath Preservation Trust has meticulously restored the building to the way it would have looked in the 18th c., when it served as a lodging for the people of fashion who came to Bath for the season. The furniture and other contents are mainly 18th c. Of particular interest are a 1798 piano by William Rolfe of Cheapside, an Aubusson carpet and a dinner service of Chamberlain's Worcester china (with its bill for £32), made for a gentleman who once lived in the Royal Crescent.

The **Royal Crescent** (John Wood II, 1767-74) is one of the great set pieces of European architecture, in which parkland sweeps up into a perfect harmony of sky and stone. Thirty identical houses, each 50ft high, make up the 500-ft Crescent. The ground floor design is simple; the first and second storeys are elaborated by an order of 114 columns, each 20ft high. The Crescent is unusual in that it forms a semi-ellipse with the end frontages in full view – unlike other, shallower crescents. A ha-ha runs across the grassland in front – a reminder of days when sheep had to be prevented from straying up from the fields below.

Walk around the Crescent, then turn right into Marlborough Buildings. Having seen the back of the Royal Crescent, one can fully appreciate how Bath's great façades are in fact shams. Each frontage has been designed to please the architect, while the remainder of the building has been custom-built to the needs of the purchaser – the result being, in most cases, haphazard. Turn right into Crescent Lane and left into *St James's*

inspiration in the Roman Colosseum, but bearing in mind his building's domestic function, he turned it to face inward instead of outward. Even more cleverly, he designed the structure in three segments so that at each of the three approaches one is met by an unbroken sweeping facade. The curved frontage consists of tiers of Roman Doric, Ionic and Corinthian three-quarter columns rising one above the other, surmounted by a parapet decorated with stone acorns linking back to the Bladud legend. The ground-floor frieze is carved with ornamental subjects. The circular central area was originally paved and cobbled throughout so that nothing would

Lansdown Crescent

Square (John Palmer, 1790-93). With its level N and S sides and its flanking E and W sides stepped down the hill, St James's resembles Queen Square; it is, however, smaller and less impressive.

Take the NW diagonal exit and turn left along Park Place into Cavendish Place (John Pinch I, 1808-16). Then continue along Cavendish Road. To the right is *Cavendish Crescent* (John Pinch I and II, 1817-30). At the crossroads, Sion Hill leads away left to *Sion Hill Place* (John Pinch I, 1818-20) the last of Bath's fine terraces to have been built.

Still keeping to the Cavendish Crescent side of the road, cross Sion Hill and climb the three flights of steps opposite the General Stores. At the top *Somerset Place* (John Eveleigh, 1793), with its unusual broken pediment, forms part of the serpentine sweep that gives **Lansdown Crescent** (John Palmer, 1789-93) its extraordinary grace. Flanked on each side by Lansdown Place West and Lansdown Place East, the Crescent has been built on a steep and uneven hillside, giving magnificent views of the city and surrounding hills. Wrought iron overthrows and lampholders lend an air of delicacy which makes it almost magical at dusk when the lights are switched on. The art connoisseur William Beckford built the connecting bridge over Upper Lansdown Mews when he moved into Nos 19 and 20.

Lansdown Place East forms a junction with the Lansdown Road. Up the hill to the left can be glimpsed **St Stephen's Church** (James Wilson, 1840-5). Its polygonal-pinnacled W tower, a bizarre example of Gothic Revival, makes the church a distinctive Bath landmark. Turning right into the Lansdown Road, walk down to the road junction. Take the second exit on the left into *Camden Crescent* (John Eveleigh, 1788). The Crescent's design is old-fashioned for its time, echoing as it does the N side of Queen Square. What distinguishes it architecturally is the odd number of columns in the centre pavilion (five), and the elephant crests over the doorways – the insignia of Charles Pratt, Marquess of Camden. The Crescent commands an extensive view of the city below, taking in on the skyline (from left to right) Brown's Folly, Sham Castle and Prior Park. Beyond the Crescent in Camden Road there are several other fine terraces built later.

Returning to Lansdown Road, continue downhill, then take a right turn into Julian Road. On the right, up a slope, stands the **Camden Works Museum**. The entire works, formerly owned by a Victorian brass founder, engineer and aerated water manufacturer, has now been restored to working order. The exhibits – among them a wood-turning lathe and a carbonating pump for ginger beer – give a good impression of a provincial family business in the 19th c. A section of stone-mine conveys some idea of the method by which the city was built. The museum also has changing exhibitions.

Cross the road, bear left into Rivers Street, left down Russell Street, right into Bennett Street and right again into Circus Place. The **Bath Carriage Museum** stands on the corner, housed in stables and coach houses that once belonged to residents of The Circus. It is the finest museum of its kind in the country. Among the exhibits can be seen the Royal Mail Coach which ran between Bristol, Bath and London; an original Bath chair; an early carriage used by Queen Victoria and Prince Albert; and a wheeled carriage once owned by Cobbs, Bath's leading baker. Carriage rides are available.

From Circus Place, cross Bennett Street and walk down the pedestrian precinct. The main entrance to the **Assembly Rooms** (NT) is on the left. Formerly known as the Upper Rooms (thus distinguishing them from the Lower Rooms SE of the Abbey in Terrace Walk) the Rooms (John Wood II, 1769-71) were purpose-built to provide evening assemblies and balls for visitors occupying the new upper reaches of the city. A square, plain building, the Rooms' main entrance is

Bath Carriage Museum

through the three-bay portico with Doric columns supporting a triangular pediment; rising behind are the twin blocks housing the Ball Room and Tea Rooms. On the N front a projecting Doric colonnade extends across the whole façade. The S front is divided into three storeys with plain windows on the ground floor, large ornate windows on the first floor and above, simple square window-lights.

To the left of the Entrance Hall is the 100ft *Ball Room* – the largest 18th-c. room in Bath. The semi-circular recess was for musicians. There are no ground-floor windows, since the room was used only in the evening. At first floor level is an order of Corinthian columns, their capitals linked by garlands, while from the coved ceiling hang five magnificent chandeliers. Turn right into the *Octagon*, originally designed as a card room; then on into the *Card Room*, added in 1777 to give more space. Finally, walk back through the Octagon to the *Tea Room*. Like the Ball Room, the Tea Room has plain lower walls, an order of columns and a high coved ceiling, here decorated with a pattern of broad ribs. A tea bar stood behind the colonnade at the W end.

The Rooms were virtually destroyed by bombs in 1942, but have now been rebuilt by the National Trust and painted in their original pastel shades. They are now used for receptions, antique fairs and tea dances.

The **Museum of Costume** was established in the remainder of the building in 1959 to display Mrs Doris Langley Moore's remarkable collection of historic costumes. The exhibition begins with a rare silver tissue dress of the 1660s – the earliest complete costume of its kind – and continues up to the present day. In the Panorama Room group scenes are set against Bath backgrounds, from the Regency period onwards. Other displays include a large range of underwear and coronation robes. All the great designers are represented, with changing displays of their work. The Museum stays up to the minute by annually choosing a top fashion journalist to select the Dress of the Year from a leading designer.

Leaving the Museum, turn left into Alfred Street and right down Lansdown Road. At the crossroads, The **Paragon** (Thomas Warr Atwood, 1770) curves away to the left; this fine sweep of houses has a cliff-like appearance seen from behind and below in Walcot Street. Halfway along is the *Countess of Huntingdon Chapel* (1765). Selina, Countess of Huntingdon, became an early Methodist convert and had the chapel built so that preachers such as John Wesley could come and address the city's fashionable congregations. A picturesque neo-Gothic manse in the courtyard screens the chapel. At the far end of the Paragon on the right stands the classical **St Swithin's Church** (1777-90), built by Thomas Jelly and John Palmer. The tower has a square base surmounted by a circular lantern and slender spire. The interior has galleries on three sides and six Ionic columns supporting the roof. Jane Austen's father (d. 1804) was curate here. He later married here, and is buried in the churchyard. Also buried here is Fanny Burney, her husband Gen. D'Arblay and their son.

Returning to the crossroads, turn right into Broad Street, with its interesting mixture of buildings, some dating from the 16th and 17th c. On the right, **King Edward's School** (Thomas Jelly, 1752) was built to house the Free Grammar School founded in 1553 under Edward VI. It is a handsome building with the City arms carved on the pediment. Further down on the left, *The Saracen's Head* (1713) is, with *No 38*, one of the street's two remaining gabled buildings. Next door, **St Michael's Church** (George Philip Manners, 1835-7) stands at the corner of Broad Street and Walcot Street. Thought to have been inspired by Salisbury Cathedral and built in the Early English style, it replaced a Georgian church, itself on the site of the medieval St Michael-extra-Muros.

Turn right into Green Street. A right turn leads back to Milsom Street.

Bowood House (see p. 57)

Bradford-on-Avon (see p. 58)   Opposite: Cheddar Gorge (see p. 61)

Gazetteer

excluding City of Bath (p.28)

Map references after place names
refer to map inside back cover
Populations over 10,000 shown
EC: Early Closing MD: Market Day

This includes information on on the location, history and main features of the places of interest in the region. Visiting hours for all places open to the public are shown in 'The Best of the Region'. Asterisks indicate references to other Gazetteer entries.

Glastonbury Tor

Alton Barnes & Alton Priors 3D
Wilts. Twin villages off A361, 6m E of Devizes

These two villages appear to be one, with cottages – some cob and thatch – scattered around fields and a stream. Located on the Ridgeway which descends from here to the Vale of Pewsey, this was the site of a Saxon settlement. **St Mary's Church** in Alton Barnes has Saxon origins; its tiny nave is only 25 x 15ft. There are several 18th-c. features: wall panelling, a gallery and a three-decker pulpit. Wall tablets commemorate two of Wiltshire's more illustrious vicars – William Crowe (public orator of Oxford University) who used to walk to Oxford from here, and his successor Augustus Hare, a benefactor of the village.

½m S on the road to Woodborough is **Honey Street**, once a depot on the Kennet and Avon Canal. *The Barge* inn is a picturesque reminder of the wharf's bustling life in Victorian times. From the hump-backed bridge the *White Horse* can be seen on Walker's Hill, 1m N of the villages. The story goes that it was cut by a farmer, at the beginning of the last century, in order to make his home village as famous as Marlborough and Cherhill. The barrow on the crest of the hill above the horse is known as *Adam's Grave*. As the name of the hill suggests, this makes a fine walk, with superb views across the Vale to Salisbury Plain.

There are many other points of interest in the area. W of the White Horse is *Milk Hill*, a nature reserve with rare chalkland flora. An Iron Age site, consisting of a small circular enclosure with the remains of hut platforms, was found here. To the E of the Marlborough road, 1¼m NE of the villages, is *Knap Hill*, whose summit is encircled by the remains of a Neolithic causewayed camp *c.* 2760BC.

Avebury 2D
Wilts. Village and prehistoric stone circle on A361, 1m N of A4, 26m NE of Bath. Inf: Tel (06723) 425

Avebury Circle (NT) is one of the most important Early Bronze Age sites in Europe. It is believed to have been built by the Beaker people *c.* 1800 BC, which makes it about 200 years earlier than the main phase of building at Stonehenge. Each of its sarsen stones – some of them 20ft high and weighing 40 tons – has been sunk deep into the solid chalk. These stones are a form of natural sandstone which occurs as boulders on the surface of the Marlborough Downs; 'sarsen' means 'saracen' or foreign, as distinguished from the indigenous chalk of that area. Within the circle, enclosing nearly 30 acres, stand the remains of two smaller circles of upright stones, while around it runs a trench. There are four entrances: from the S entrance a double line of standing stones known as *West Kennet Avenue* leads away for 1½m to The Sanctuary on Overton Hill. Concrete plinths mark the gaps where stones have been removed in the past.

Just beyond the Circle stands the National Trust Information Centre and shop, leading into a yard with a pond. To one side is the Great Barn housing the *Folk Life Museum*, with displays of farm equipment and historic photographs of local interest. On the far side of the yard is the Alexander Keiller Museum. (**Avebury Museum**). Opened in 1938 to house the material excavated by the founder at Windmill Hill, the museum also has finds from Silbury Hill, Avebury and West Kennet Long Barrow.

St James's Church, near the museum, was founded in Saxon times. Although restored in 1879, much of its original work remains, including two windows. The door and geometrically carved font are Norman; the tower is 14th-c. Some of the stone used to build the church was removed from Avebury Circle. A path from the churchyard leads across the River Kennet via New Bridge giving a good view of Silbury Hill and Avebury · Trusloe; this row of late 17th-c. and Georgian houses includes *Trusloe Manor*, a stone-faced 17th-c. house.

A pathway beside Avebury Museum leads to **Avebury Manor**, a pleasant Elizabethan house with panelled rooms, early oak furniture and plasterwork ceilings. The house was built on the site of a monastery by Sir William Sharington (*c.* 1550) at about the same time that he was buying Lacock Abbey. During the Civil War it belonged to a royalist, Sir John Stawell, whose memory is recalled by the haunted Cavalier Bedroom. Most of the major alterations were made to the house following its sale to Sir Richard Holford in 1696. A parapet was added to the S wall of the Mervyn Wing, a curved wall built to enclose the SW garden, and the Elizabethan Great Hall was redecorated as a dining-room in preparation for a visit by Queen Anne. A topiary garden lies behind the house, with fountains and peacocks.

1m NW of Avebury is *Windmill Hill*, another important site with Neolithic earthworks and barrows.

Avoncliff 3C

Wilts. Industrial site and picturesque spot off B3108, 7m SE of Bath

Standing on the line between Bath and Bradford-on-Avon, Avoncliff station has one of the shortest platforms in the country – only one carriage long. The fine **Aqueduct**, built by John Rennie in the early 1800s, has been re-lined by volunteers from the Kennet and Avon Trust. The *Old Court*, built around three sides of a courtyard, was once a workhouse. Behind it stands a chapel and a domed weaver's drying house. *The Cross Guns*, a charming 17th-c. riverside pub, is a popular stopping-place for visitors who have just completed the walk along the canal from the Tithe Barn at Bradford-on-Avon.

Babington 3B

Somerset. Village off A362, 12m S of Bath

A tree-lined drive leads off the main road to the manor house and church – all that remains of the medieval village. *Babington House* was built *c.* 1700. Its original façade has two storeys and seven bays; the side with a big bow was added in 1790. Across the lawn stands the 18th-c. **St Margaret's Church**. Reputedly the work of John Strahan, the church retains its original panelling, box pews and small octagonal turret.

Glastonbury Abbey (see p. 70)

Wells Cathedral interior and (above) view from Bishop's Palace (see p. 89)

Badminton House
See *Great Badminton*.

Bathampton   2B (Bath area)
Avon. Village off A36, 2m NE of Bath

St Nicholas' Church, dominating the village, attracts many Australian visitors. Buried here is Admiral Arthur Phillip, the founder of Australia. He led the first party of settlers to Australia in 1788 and eventually became Governor of New South Wales. Recently a new chapel was dedicated to him. The chancel and Perpendicular W tower are 13th-c., the rest of the building mainly 19th-c. There are three medieval stone monuments: a 14th-c. lady at one window, her knight at another, and the figure of a bishop (said to be Norman) in a recess under the E window. In the S aisle can be seen memorials to the family of Ralph Allen, the famous Bath stonemerchant.

Opposite the church by the Kennet and Avon Canal stands *The George* inn, originally a medieval monastic building. A popular local haunt, the pub makes a welcome ending to a canal walk (see p. 17). Nearby, also on the canal, stands Harbutt's plasticine factory. William Harbutt invented plasticine here in 1897 and it now constitutes the local industry.

N of the village on the road to Batheaston there is a weir and an arched toll-bridge over the river. The toll-house still exacts a few pence from cars crossing the bridge. Beyond stands *The Old Mill* – now a hotel.

Batheaston   2B
Avon. Village on A4, 2m NE of Bath

Batheaston's **High Street**, now part of the noisy A4, has some notable 18th-c. buildings, including *Batheaston House* (1712) and *The Lamb and Flag* inn.

A left turning off the High Street leads to *North End*, a more peaceful part of the village (for walk to Little Solsbury Hill, see p. 18). On the left is **St John Baptist's Church**, with its large buttressed W tower (94ft high), thought to be 15th-c.; the rest of the building is mainly 19th-c. The octagonal font dates back to c. 1700. Opposite the church are a number of attractive houses, among them two of the late 17th c. Further along stands *Eagle House*, which John Wood the Elder built for himself in 1727, in the Palladian style.

Bathford   2B
Avon. Village off A4, 3m NE of Bath

Stone Georgian houses and cottages cluster round **St Swithin's Church**, with its large 18th-c. W tower. Heavily restored in the 19th c., the church retains a Norman font and finely carved Jacobean pulpit. In nearby Pump Lane are two cottages with straight gables and mullioned windows (1662), and a coaching inn, *The Crown*.

Beside the church a narrow lane leads up a steep slope to the nature reserve at Mountain Wood. From here there is a footpath up to *Brown's Folly*, built by Mr Wade Brown in 1840 to give work to local craftsmen during a period of depression after the Napoleonic Wars. From the folly there is a scenic view over the Limpley Stoke valley. (See also *Walk 6*, p. 18).

Battlesbury Camp   4C
Wilts. Ancient site off A36, 2m NE of Warminster

The site is reached through Warminster: left off the A36 into Woodcock Road, then right into Battlesbury Road, whence a short walk leads to the site. Covering 25 acres, the late Iron Age hill fort has double defences and entrances protected by outworks to the E and W. Over the centuries ploughing has reduced the size of the ramparts and interior. Just N of the fort, traces of an Iron Age settlement have been found.

Beckford's Tower   2B
Avon. Folly and museum off Lansdown Road, 1m N of Bath

Art connoisseur, millionaire and eccentric, William Beckford commissioned H.E. Goodridge to build the Tower in 1825-26. Originally it marked the N limit of his estate, which stretched up from his home in Lansdown Crescent. Although not as outlandish as his earlier master-folly – Fonthill Abbey – the Tower is extraordinary. 154ft high, it is square-built with an octagonal lantern inspired by the Lysicrates Monument in Athens. At the top is a belvedere; at the foot, a small two-storeyed house with a one-storey addition. Part of this is now a small museum of Beckfordiana.

The gates and wall of *Lansdown Cemetery*, in which the Tower stands, are also by Goodridge. Both Beckford and Goodridge are buried in the cemetery; Beckford's tomb surrounded by a deep trench. A smaller tower built by Beckford stands in the grounds of Kingswood School further downhill.

Beckington 3C
Somerset. Village on A36, 12m SE of Bath

The village's fine 16th-c. stone houses are a reminder of its past as a busy clothing centre. At Castle Corner, on the main Frome road, stands *The Castle* – not a castle at all, but a late-16th-c. house, three-storeyed with three steep gables and two rounded towers. Further along the road is the similarly misnamed *Abbey*. Founded in 1502 as the Hospital of the Augustinian canons, it is a large building retaining some 16th-c. work. Inside on the first floor is one of the most ornate barrel-vaulted plaster ceilings in Somerset.

The Woolpack inn stands on a corner nearby. **St George's Church**, up Church Hill to the left, is largely Perpendicular, but with one of the county's largest and finest Norman towers. The great carved roof of the nave and SE chapel were probably endowed by John Compton, a 15th-c. cloth merchant. The monument to the poet Samuel Daniel (d. 1619) is designed – unusually for its time – in the classical style. A memorial to John Seyntmaur (d. 1485) is set in the chancel floor; his name is a variant spelling of Seymour.

Thomas Bekynton, Henry VI's Chancellor and later Bishop of Bath and Wells, was born in the village.

Seymour Court, home of the Seymour family, lies 1m NE of the village; a partly 16th-c. house, it was built by Protector Somerset, brother of Jane Seymour, third wife of Henry VIII. (Somerset ruled for the boy king Edward VI.)

Berkley 3C
Somerset. Village off A36, 14m SE of Bath

The **Church of St Mary the Virgin** is considered one of the finest Georgian churches in the county. Probably designed by Thomas Prowse during the late 1740s, the church is built on a square ground-plan with four giant columns supporting the central dome; its roof is decorated with plaster scrolls and crowned with a small glass cupola. There are several monuments to the Newburgh family.

The *Manor House* behind the church was the home of the Newburghs in the 17th c., and of Thomas Prowse during the 18th c. The elegant Georgian façade was designed by Nathaniel Ireson.

Biddestone 2C
Wilts. Village off A4 at Corsham, 11m NE of Bath

One of the area's prettiest villages, with some perfect 17th and 18th-c. stone buildings. On the outskirts to the E is the *Manor House*, a gabled house with mullioned windows, stables and a gazebo set on a wall. Other attractive buildings are *Pool Farmhouse*, also with a gazebo, *The White Horse* inn and *Willow House* with its pedimented front.

St Nicholas' Church is unusual in having no tower: instead, there is a 13th-c. bell-turret. The church's Norman origin is still evident in the doorway, chancel windows and font. The gallery and box pews were built in the 17th c. to accommodate parishioners from nearby Slaughterford whose church was destroyed by Cromwell's troops. Note the separate stairways by which the newcomers were segregated from the locals.

Bowood 2C
Wilts Historic house off A4, 4m SE of Chippenham

The home of the Lansdowne family, Bowood is one of Wiltshire's most famous stately homes. The present house is the surviving part of the original 18th-c. 'Great House', demolished in 1955.

The S range was designed by Robert Adam as an orangery, and is now the *Picture Gallery*. At the E end of the range is Robert Adam's *Library* and the laboratory where Dr. Joseph Priestley discovered oxygen gas in 1774. Leading off the Picture Gallery is the *Chapel* designed by C.R. Cockerell in 1821. At the W end of the range is the *Sculpture Gallery* housing a display of ancient Greek and Roman statuary, and on the floor above are exhibition rooms showing exquisite 18th-c. family costumes, including Lord Byron's Albanian dress, displays of Victoriana and Indiana and an important collection of watercolours and drawings by famous 19th-c. artists.

The **Park** – 1000 acres laid out by Capability Brown – is one of his finest works of landscaping. The 40-acre lake is set among fields and beech woods. The Lake Walk leads to the Cascade, designed by the Hon C. Hamilton in 1785, a Hermit's Cave and the Doric Temple. The gardens are renowned for their spring daffodils and summer roses, while the Arboretum contains overs 200 varieties of splendid specimens of trees and shrubs. Robert Adam's magnificent *Mausoleum* dominates the spectacular Rhododendron Gardens, 50 acres of towering rhododendrons open mid-May to mid-Jun in a separate area of the park. There is an adventure playground for children.

Box 2C
Wilts. Village on A4, 6m NE of Bath

This village is the site of the Box railway tunnel, one of Brunel's greatest engineering achievements on the Great Western Railway. The 3212yd-long tunnel, linking Box and Corsham, was completed in 1840 as part of the final stage of the London to Bristol railway.

On the left, entering the village from Bath, stands *The Blind House*, an old lock-up; nearby is a 19th-c. school with a clock tower. A left turn down Church Lane leads to a precinct of older houses, including a tall, 17th-c. school building with mullioned windows. The **Church of St Thomas of Canterbury** has a 15th-c. tower rising in open arcading, topped by a spire. Among its treasures are a 15th-c. font decorated with roses

and a 12th-c. effigy set in a vaulted recess. During the 19th c. the church was enlarged at the railway company's expense for the men working on the tunnel.

Leaving Box on the Chippenham road, the impressive entrance to **Box Tunnel** can be seen on the right; its sides curve into the hillside and a balustrade runs along the top.

Bradford-on-Avon 3C
Wilts. Town on A363, 6m E of Bath

Set on steep hillsides with unusual perspectives, the town has many fine houses built by prosperous cloth merchants in the 15th-17th c.

The six-arched town **bridge** retains two of its original medieval arches; the remainder was rebuilt in the 17th c. The curious central domed building was formerly a chapel, where pilgrims to Glastonbury stopped to pray; in the 17th c. it was converted into a lock-up.

S of the bridge stands a gabled 17th-c. house, now *Spindles Restaurant*, and next door the 18th-c. *Georgian Wine Lodge*. Down the Frome Road a signpost points to Barton Farm and the 14th-c. **Tithe Barn**. The second largest in the country, the barn is 168 x 30ft with four porches and 14 bays. (From the barn there is a pleasant 1m canal-side walk to Avoncliff.)

Returning to the bridge, recross it into Market Street. On the left in Church Street is *The Swan Hotel*, a Georgian building with three bays. Nearby stand the 15th-c. *Church Hall*, the early Georgian *Druce's Hill House* and the 17th-c. *Chantry*.

Up the hill, next to the parish church, is the town's greatest treasure – the tiny Saxon **Church of St Lawrence**. In use as a cottage, this was discovered by accident in 1858 between an adjoining school and factory. The church was founded by St Aldhelm, Bishop of Malmesbury, as part of a monastery known to have existed in 705AD. The church's only decorations are two angels sculpted in low relief above the chancel arch. The **Church of Holy Trinity** nearby is of Norman foundation, with Norman win-

Stonehenge (see p. 86)

dows in the chancel and above the S porch. Returning to Market Street, a turning up through The Shambles with its timber-framed houses leads into Silver Street. Several elegant Georgian houses stand on the road leading up to *The Hall* – a magnificent Jacobean house built in 1610.

Bratton Castle
See *Westbury*

Broadleas Gardens
See *Devizes*

Bromham 2C
Wilts. Village off A342, 5m NW of Devizes

In the churchyard of **St Nicholas' Church** the poet Thomas Moore (d.1852) lies buried, his grave marked by a Celtic cross. Nearby, in the NE corner of the yard, there is an old timber *lock-up*. The church itself has a tall 13th-c. Early English tower with a Perpendicular spire; the rest of the building is mainly Perpendicular. Inside, the Beauchamp Chapel (1492) has three elaborately decorated bays. The E window of the chapel is particularly fine: dedicated to Elizabeth Morris, it is the work of William Morris, based on figures designed by Edward Burne-Jones. Two especially grand tombs commemorate Sir Roger Tocotes (d. 1457) and Sir Edward Baynton (d. 1578); there is also a Purbeck marble monument to Elizabeth Beauchamp (d. 1492).

At Sloperton, 2m N on the A3102, stands *Sloperton Cottage*, Thomas Moore's home from 1818-52, where he was visited by Samuel Rogers and Washington Irving.

Burrington Combe 3A
Avon. Gorge on B3134, 10m NW of Wells

The main road runs through the gorge which, although not as grand as Cheddar, is perhaps more attractive. Black Down, rising 1065ft above the Combe, is one of the highest peaks on Mendip. It was here that the 19th-c. curate Augustus Toplady composed the hymn *Rock of Ages Cleft For Me* on a rock face, while sheltering from a storm.

Calne 2C
Wilts. Town on A4, 19m NE of Bath

As it enters the town the main road opens out into a broad space known as The Strand. At one corner stands the Town Hall and clock tower, and a large Georgian coaching inn, *The Lansdowne Arms* (see p. 15). Opposite are the red-brick blocks of the sausage factory (now closed down) – the successor to Calne's original wool industry.

Church Street leads off between the factory buildings into a much older part of Calne. Half-way along on the left stands **St Mary's Church**, set on a green sward with fine yew hedges. The church was built between the 12th and 15th c.; the present 17th-c. tower is attributed to Inigo Jones. Battlements, pinnacles and great windows make St Mary's a noble building. Inside, there is an impressive Norman nave with ornamented arches and a 15th-c. clerestory, rising to a fine timber roof.

Further along Church Street on the right *Wiltshire Tracklements* sells its own brands of delicious preserves and the famous Urchfont mustards.

Proclamation Steps – where royal proclamations are read – lead from the church down the slope to Mill Street. On the left is *Calne Mill* and just beyond, a path beside the River Marden leads to *Doctor's Pond*. In this peaceful backwater the scientist Joseph Priestley collected gases from which he isolated oxygen while working for the Marquis of Lansdowne at Bowood (1772-78).

Returning to the church, a narrow street, The Green, curves round to the *Dr Townson Almshouses* – eight diminutive houses with latticed windows and dwarf-size doors. The street opens out into **The Green**, with a number of fine Georgian houses. These include *Joseph Priestley's House* (marked with a plaque), the old *Boys' and Girls' Schools*, and *The White Hart Hotel* facing on to the main Marlborough road. *Adam House*, with its three bays and Venetian window, is believed to have been the home of Robert Adam while he worked on the rebuilding of **Bowood House*, 2m SW of Calne.

Castle Combe
Wilts Village off A420, 13m NE of Bath

2C

For some years dubbed 'the prettiest village in England', Castle Combe can afford to be a trifle self-conscious. The film *Dr Doolittle* was made here in 1966, and ever since the village has attracted crowds of visitors. To keep the place unspoilt, cars must be left in a car park from which it is a short walk down to the village.

The cluster of mellowed Cotswold buildings set on a hillside is dominated by the fine **St Andrew's Church**. Although greatly restored in 1851, the church (originally 13th-c.) has kept its early 15th-c. tower; 76 arches run around the top, and there are pinnacled buttresses. On the roof of the nave can be seen the carved shuttle and scissors mark of the cloth merchants who built the tower, a reminder of the village's prosperous past. Inside, the chancel still retains its original 13th-c. wall and font with stone book-rest. The roof is handsomely vaulted, and there is an oak screen with traceried panels and an oak-panelled pulpit. St Andrew's boasts one of the smallest priest's doors in the country – 5ft high and just over 2ft wide. In the N aisle is the 13th-c. tomb of Sir Walter de Dunstanville, whose effigy is in chain armour, with angels at the head and a dog at the feet. It was this knight who built the castle– long since disappeared – from which the village took its name.

In front of the church, set on great stone steps, stands the covered cross marking the site of an ancient wool market. From here the main street, lined with stone-built gabled cottages, descends to the fast-flowing Bybrook, spanned by a three-arched bridge. On the other side of the hill stands what was once the manor house rebuilt by the Victorians. It is now *The Manor Hotel*, comfortably set in a screened setting of trees and spreading lawns.

Chalcot House
Wilts. Historic house off A3098, 15m SE of Bath

3C

This small Palladian manor house is finely situated, with views to Salisbury Plain and Longleat. Roman remains have been found in the garden, including several thousand coins dating back to 270AD. Formerly a medieval manor, the house was rebuilt in the 17th-18th c. In 1872 an extensive restoration was carried out by J.P. St Aubyn, who added a rear wing. Much of his work was subsequently removed when the house was modernised (1971). Visitors to Chalcot (open only during afternoons in Aug) are conducted around by the owner. The ballroom should be noted for its fine plasterwork.

Cheddar
Somerset. Village on A371 8m NW of Wells

3A

Nowadays, people tend to associate the pretty village of Cheddar with cheese and strawberries. Back in Saxon times, however, Cheddar played a far more important role in the life of the nation. There was once a royal palace and parliament (known as a *witan*) where the Kings of Wessex School now stands. The faint outline of wooden buildings can be traced in the school grounds, and the ruined *Chapel of St Columbanus*, a notable 6th-c. Celtic monk, can still be seen there.

The village centre is dominated by the imposing 110ft tower of **St Andrew's Church**. Of Saxon foundation, it was rebuilt during the 14th c. Its S chapel is dedicated to St Nectan who, like St Columbanus, was a 6th-c. monk belonging to a Celtic religious order. In the chancel stands the tomb of Sir Thomas Cheddar (d. 1443) and his wife.

The medieval market cross and the 16th-c. colonnade around it have been greatly restored. Nearby, in Lower North Street, stands the white-washed cottage that was once the home of Hannah More. An 18th-c. philanthropist, she did a great deal for Mendip people and in 1789 founded Cheddar's first day school.

Cheddar Gorge (NT) One of the greatest natural fissures in Britain, the Gorge begins near the village and runs almost to the top of Mendip. About 400 caves or holes are known to riddle its cliffs. Of these, Gough's and Cox's

Caves are the best known. Walking up from the village, a number of attractions lie along the foot of the Gorge:

Gough's Motor Museum More than 30 historic cars and motor cycles – from a 1912 Buick to the Duke of Windsor's 1933 Humber Snipe 80 – are on show.

Jacob's Ladder 300 steep steps up the cliff-face lead to a tower which gives a spectacular view out over the Mendips, the Somerset Moors, the Quantocks, Exmoor and the Bristol Channel.

Waterfall Grotto A man-made display of falling water duplicates the activities of the river which originally formed the caves.

Cox's Cave In 1837 a Mr Cox, while hacking at the rock face to make room for a new cart shed, discovered a huge cave of stalactites. The cave was found to be a geological museum of the Ice Age and Old Stone Age, with extraordinary limestone formations. Now, each formation has been skillfully lit with plain white light to show off the brilliant variety of colours naturally caused by minerals present in the rock. The formations are appropriately named according to their shape and colour, with titles such as the Peal of Bells, the Mermaid and the Transformation Scene.

Cheddar Caves Museum The museum is divided into two sections: the N Room exhibits finds in the Caves from Old Stone Age to Medieval times, including the renowned 10,000-year-old skeleton known as Cheddar Man; the S Room's theme is 'Man on Mendip' and includes illustrations and a diorama of human-kind from Old Stone Age to 19th-c. times, with a reproduction of an early cave family.

Gough's Cave Discovered in 1877, the Cave contains the skeleton pit which divers have explored to a depth of 74ft. It was here that they found the skeleton of Cheddar Man. Stalactite formations in this cave are even more dramatic than those in Cox's Cave, with names such as the Fairy Grotto, Organ Pipes, Pixie Forest and King Solomon's Temple.

Black Rock Nature Reserve Walk This 1½m circular walk through woodland and down (NT) starts at the N end of the Gorge.

Cherhill 2D
Wilts. Village on A4, 22m NE of Bath

The sprawling village of Cherhill lies at the foot of the Downs. **St James's Church** is linked to the manor house by a public footpath. The church's exterior is 15th-c., finishing in a Perpendicular tower; its interior is mostly Victorian.

The village is dominated by the 130-ft-high **White Horse** cut into the hillside on the opposite side of the main road. Dr Christopher Alsop, a Calne physician, designed the horse in 1780; he is said to have stood a mile away from the site shouting instructions to his men through a loudspeaker as they worked. Above the White Horse towers *Lansdowne Column*, put up by the 3rd Marquis of Lansdowne in honour of an ancestor.

Oldbury Castle, ¾m SE of the village, is an unfinished Iron Age hill fort enclosing 25 acres, with a SE entrance. Iron Age and Roman objects have been found on the site.

Chew Magna 2A
Avon. Village on B3130, 12m W of Bath

Like most of its neighbouring villages, Chew Magna was once a centre for clothing and for the manufacture of ruddle to mark sheep. The handsome Georgian houses set around the main street recall its 18th-c. prosperity.

Overlooking the village green is the 15th-c. **St Andrew's Church**, with a pinnacled tower. Before entering the church note the old *Church House* (c. 1510) with the arms of the St Loe family above the entrance. The St Loes were the local squires who lived at Sutton Court 2m SE of the village.

Inside the church, the most striking feature is the painted medieval rood screen, restored in the 19th c. The church's most impressive tomb bears the oak figure of Sir John de Hauteville (14th-c.), one of the country's few remaining medieval painted effigies. Sir

John was said to have thrown the Hauteville Quoit (see *Stanton Drew*). Next is the tomb of the squire Sir John St Loe (d. 1448), a giant of a man (7ft 4ins), together with his wife. In the Lady Chapel can be seen the tomb of Edward Baber, an Elizabethan JP, together with his wife. A wall plaque commemorates Thomas Minor, who sailed to Salem, Massachusetts in 1629 and founded Stonington, Connecticut. The N chapel is full of memorials to the Strachey family who succeeded the St Loes at Sutton Court, their most famous member being the historian and critic Lytton Strachey.

Chew Court stands behind a sandstone wall at the E end of the church. Built in the early 16th c for Bishop John Clerk, it once formed part of the estate of the Bishop of Bath and Wells, and manorial courts were held here.

S of the village, a fine late 15th-c. bridge with three pointed arches spans the River Chew. There is a pleasant 1m walk from the village S to the *Chew Valley lake*.

Chew Stoke   3A
Avon. Village on B3114, 13m SW of Bath

Set beside Chew Valley Lake, Chew Stoke offers good fishing. During the 18th c. the Bilbie family of bell-founders and clockmakers brought renown to the village.

The originally medieval church is now largely Victorian. More interesting is the *Old Rectory*, which stands at the crossroads. Its front wall is decorated with 20 stone panels of angels: they include the arms of St Loe, a prominent local family, the name of the rector who built it, John Barry, and the date, 1529. A pleasant group of restored cottages stands beside the bridge over the stream.

Chew Valley Lake   3A
Avon

Created in 1955 to provide Bristol with extra water, this is one of the largest reservoirs in southern England. Stocked with trout, it is popular with anglers and offers good sailing.

Chewton Mendip   3A/3B
Somerset. Village on A39, 6m NE of Wells

A former lead-mining village, Chewton Mendip stands at the source of the River Chew. The **Church of St Mary Magdalene** has a splendid 126ft-high tower, famous throughout Somerset. Originally Saxon, the church has been often rebuilt, first by the Normans, then by Carthusian monks in the 15th-16th c., and finally in the 19th c. The Lady Chapel contains a 15th-c. tomb with carved figures of Sir Henry Fitzroger and his wife. Opposite them on the wall is a white marble portrait of Frances Countess of Waldegrave – a famous society hostess at whose London home Mr Gladstone met his Liberal supporters. A *fryd* stool is set on one side of the chancel; it dates from the time when a criminal might take sanctuary in a church. Further along the wall is the church's most beautiful window, stained in blue and white; the portrait of a tearful Virgin Mary on one side has been restored from medieval fragments. Just outside the church stands a 14th-c. *Cross* – one of only four medieval crosses in Somerset.

On the outskirts of the village a sign points away from the main road to *Chewton Cheese Dairy*. Visitors can watch cheese and butter being made by traditional methods every morning; the dairy also has a small shop selling butter, cheese, eggs and other produce.

Chippenham   2C
Wilts. Pop 19,000. 13m NE of Bath (A4). EC Wed MD Fri. Inf: Tel (0249) 57733

The name 'Chippenham' was first recorded in 853 as the site of the marriage between the King of Mercia and the sister of Alfred the Great. Later, Alfred is said to have bequeathed the town to his daughter Elfrida. Like so many other Wiltshire towns, Chippenham was once a prosperous wool centre with 12 mills. Its red-brick houses reflect a period during the 19th c. when, with the coming of the Great Western Railway, its cloth factories and iron foundries were known nationally.

The old town is centred round the Market Place which leads, at one end,

'Strawberry Hill Gothick' frontage. Most of this later had to be pulled down, to be replaced by Thomas Bellamy's more solid, Victorian structure in 1845.

The Methuen collection, with later additions, now includes works by Fra Filippo Lippi, Breughel, Caravaggio, Rubens, Van Dyck, Reynolds and Gainsborough, as well as a sculpture believed by some experts to be by Michelangelo. The house's furniture includes mirrors by Adam, a Cobb commode, a number of fine pieces by Chippendale, and a table by the American cabinetmaker Duncan Phyfe.

Tucked away behind the house is Capability Brown's *Bath House* – a charming 'Gothick' structure connected with the flower garden by a sloping passage opening into a 15th-c. porch. All that remains of Nash's work is a little decoration on the E front, a dairy and a quaint cottage across the lake.

Corsham's park and gardens were created by Capability Brown and later added to by Humphrey Repton. Their chief features are an artificial lake covering 13 acres, the *North Walk* (2m) which culminates in a handsome classical gateway, and exotic trees.

Devizes

3D

Wilts, Pop. 10,300. Town on A361 20m SE of Bath. Event: Carnival (last week in Aug). EC Wed, MD Thur, Sat. Inf: Tel (0380) 71279

Devizes is one of Wiltshire's oldest boroughs. Its traditional market-town atmosphere has survived despite new shopping developments, and there are still many 16th- and 17th-c. cottages to be discovered tucked away behind the main streets.

The busy Market Place is lined with a number of historic buildings, including two well-known Georgian hotels – *The Bear* and *The Black Swan*. *The Bear* was one of the most fashionable coaching inns of its time, visited by many famous people (see p.15).

The *Market Cross* which stands in the centre of Market Place has a remarkable inscription, recording a bizarre occurrence in 1753 when a marketwoman, Ruth Pierce, attempted a deceit – with fatal consequences.

Walking out of the Market Place into St John Street, the gateway and towers of **Devizes Castle** come into view down a turning to the right. The original castle on this site was Norman, built by Bishop Roger of Salisbury: the town grew up later around it. Following its virtual destruction by Oliver Cromwell's forces, the castle was finally rebuilt during the early 19th c. by the Bath architect H.E. Goodridge. The original Norman moat and mound can still be seen from outside the gate; the rest is private property.

Further down St John Street is the 18th-c. *Town Hall* (built by Thomas Baldwin of Bath), with a five-bayed frontage and Ionic columns. Through St John's Court on the right stands the Norman **St John's Church**. Like the castle, the church is believed to have been built by Bishop Roger and probably served as its chapel. Apart from the finely decorated Norman tower and the W front, which is 19th-c., most of the exterior is 15th-c. Inside, there are low Norman arches in the chancel, and a vaulted roof. The Beauchamp Chapel has a panelled Tudor ceiling. Among the memorials in the churchyard is one to Robert Merrit, his wife and three others, who drowned while boating in a pond one Sunday evening. The inscription ends with the admonition: 'Remember the Sabbath Day, to keep it holy'.

In Long Street, on the other side of the Town Hall, is the **Devizes Museum**, which contains collections of finds from the local prehistoric sites – Stonehenge, Woodhenge, the Sanctuary at Overton Hill, West Kennet Long Barrow and Silbury Hill. On the London Road (Marchant Barracks) is the *Wiltshire Regimental Museum*.

In the S of the town in Potterne Road lies **Broadleas**, an attractive garden. The dell is planted with unusual trees and shrubs, including azaleas and rhododendrons. Both the rock garden and winter garden contain many rare plants.

To the W of the town, at Caen Hill, is

the remarkable **flight of 29 locks** which raise the level of the Kennet and Avon Canal by 237ft over a distance of 2m. The locks (now being restored) are the work of John Rennie (1797-1800). For canal trips from Devizes, see p.16.

1m N of the town is *Roundway Down*, site of a bloody Civil War Battle in 1643. A determined Royalist cavalry charge here swept the Roundheads over the escarpment. A nature walk and fine views can be enjoyed.

Dodington House 1B
Avon. Historic house off A46, 10m N of Bath

Dodington is owned by the Codrington family, who were given their coat-of-arms at the time of Agincourt (1415) by Henry V. James Wyatt designed the present neo-classical building for Christopher Codrington, between 1796 and 1813.

The house has three main fronts, of different designs. The Entrance Front has a colossal Roman Corinthian portico with a curving conservatory to one side; the Terrace Front a centrepiece with attached columns and pilasters; while the East Front is simpler, with projecting bows at each end. Inside, the house is Wyatt at his most lavish, with a fine entrance hall and staircase, brass-inlaid floors, black marble, Cotswold stone, and cast-iron or brass fireplaces. There are paintings by many European masters, including Rembrandt and Titian. The basement contains an exhibition of the history of the Codrington family and the house, with Wyatt's drawings. Outside the adjoining stable block houses one of the largest collections of horse-drawn vehicles in the country – from farm carts to State coaches.

Just N of the house stands the *Dower House*, once a dairy. Nearby is Wyatt's neo-classical church building, now a brass-rubbing centre. Visitors can enjoy a carriage ride through the park to admire Capability Brown's landscaping effects: they include an ornamental Gothic cascade and a fishing house.

There is a 4-acre adventure playground with tree-houses and climbing ropes and a train ride to the lake.

Doulting 4B
Somerset. Village on A361, 2m E of Shepton Mallet

The name is synonymous with the light cream stone quarried here and used to build Wells Cathedral and Glastonbury Abbey, together with most of the buildings in the village.

St Aldhelm's Church, unlike most Somerset churches, has a spire – dating from the 15th c. – above a 13th-c. octagonal tower. The church's other outstanding feature is its beautiful 15th-c. porch with two storeys and an elegant gable. Beside the N porch stands a historic churchyard *Cross*.

Behind the former vicarage (18th-c.) a path leads downhill to *St Aldhelm's Well* – a spring recalling one of early Christianity's most famous saints. As Bishop of Sherborne and Abbot of Malmesbury, Aldhelm founded religious communities all over Dorset and Somerset until he died here in 709 AD.

The 15th-c. **Tithe Barn** standing S of the village and belonging to *Manor Farm* (17th-c.) was built by the monks of Glastonbury, who originally owned the estate. The barn has two porches on each side and a huge timbered roof.

Downside Abbey 3B
Somerset. Abbey church off A367, 11m SW of Bath

Downside, in the village of Stratton-on-the-Fosse, is the home of a Roman Catholic public school. Its community of Benedictine monks, originally from Douai in northern France, bought the 17th-c. mansion of Mount Pleasant in 1814 and commissioned H.E. Goodridge to carry out alterations.

The **Abbey Church** is a splendid example of 19th- and 20th-c. Gothic Revival architecture, including styles which range from the Early English to the Perpendicular. The church is 110yds long, the choir 74ft high. The W front is temporary; another two-and-a-half bays remain to be built, bringing the number of nave bays up to eleven. The building is rib-vaulted throughout. The firm of A. Dunn & E. Hanson designed the N transept, S transept, crossing, ambulatory and a number of radiating chapels

(1872). The chancel with its tall clerestory windows is the work of Thomas Garner (1901-5). Sir Giles Gilbert Scott was responsible for the nave (1938); he also built the upper part of the great tower, which dominates the landscape for miles around.

The Lady Chapel has an exquisitely carved roof in which the bosses represent the Virtues and the capitals the flowers which are named after the Madonna. The chapel's nine windows have some of the best-designed modern glass in the country.

Dyrham Park (NT)   2B
Avon. Historic house off A46, 8m N of Bath, 2m S of M4 (Exit 18)

Dyrham (the name means 'deer enclosure') is a strange mixture of styles: a building strangely located, too, in its narrow Cotswold valley. The old Tudor manor house, the home of the Wynter family, was transformed by William Blathwayt, Secretary of State to William III. Blathwayt married Mary Wynter, heiress to the estate, and set about rebuilding his new home between 1692 and 1704. He employed two architects: first the Frenchman S. Hauduroy, and later William Talman, deputy to Christopher Wren. The French-influenced W front (the back of the house overlooking the garden and church) was the work of Hauduroy; the classical E front and adjoining Orangery, approached through the Deer Park, was the work of Talman.

Much of the interior is unchanged since Blathwayt's time and shows a strong Dutch influence, with floors of Flemish oak, enclosed square staircases and walnut grained panelling. The embellishments are also Dutch: the blue-and-white Delftware, leather hangings, Hondecoeter bird paintings and perspective paintings by van Hoogstraeten.

Dyrham is a fine example of Baroque planning. Some of the ground floor and all of the first floor were laid out in apartments, each consisting of between eight and ten rooms. The Dyrham State Bed in the Queen Anne Room is 1705, and much of the other furniture, collected by succeeding generations, shows 18th-c. taste at its best. The Hall contains three ceiling paintings by Andrea Casali, which hung for a time in the Theatre Royal, Bath.

Dyrham's garden and park were first conceived in the Dutch style, with parterres, a canal and a cascade second only to that at Chatsworth, with 224 steps and 20ft jets. Now, only a statue of Neptune carved by John Harvey of Bath remains on the crown of the slope where the cascade once flowed. Around the turn of the 19th c. Humphrey Repton and his son were employed to landscape and 'picturesque' the grounds with cedars, broad-leafed trees and shrubs.

Behind the house is the delightful parish *Church* – almost a part of the garden. Originally Norman, it has monuments to the Blathwayt family. The tiny village of Dyrham is on the far side of the park.

Edington   3C
Wilts. Village on B3098, 4m E of Westbury. Event: Music Festival (Aug)

The **Church of St Mary, St Katherine and All Saints** is one of Wiltshire's finest churches, and the site of an annual music festival (end Aug). Founded as a priory church in 1351 by William of Edington, Bishop of Winchester and Chancellor to Edward III, the building has a cathedral-like grandeur, and shows the transition from the Decorated to the Perpendicular style. The nave ceiling and the tower crossing were added in the 17th c., the chancel ceiling in the 18th c. Both the pulpit and the altar rails are 17th-c. The building's central tower houses one of the oldest working clocks in the country. Monuments include two 14th-c. knights removed from the church at Imber (a deserted village on Salisbury Plain now used for military manoeuvres); there are also several 17th-c. memorials.

Below the church to the W stands *The Priory* on the site of its original foundation: there are fish ponds in the garden.

Farleigh Castle   3B/3C
Somerset. Castle ruins off A366, 9m SE of Bath

The castle site lies beyond Farleigh Hungerford village. Two ruined towers and exposed foundations, set among rolling hills, are all that remain of what was once an impressive fortification. Built in 1377 by Sir Thomas Hungerford, Speaker of the House of Commons, the castle was originally a rectangular structure with round towers and a large gatehouse; a hall, dining room and kitchen stood within the enclosure. Sir Thomas' son Walter, Baron Hungerford, added an outer courtyard, stables and guard rooms, taking in the area of the mid-14th-c. parish church – which then became the family's chapel.

In 1644 Parliamentary forces took the castle from the Royalists. By 1701 the building was described as 'very ruinous'. The *chapel* has a particularly interesting early 16th-c. W porch; inside is the large tomb of its founder, together with other 16th and 17th-c. family monuments.

Overlooking the ruins is *The Hungerford Arms* inn – itself several hundred years old.

Freshford
3B

Avon. Village off A36, 6m SE of Bath

One of Avon's most attractive villages, Freshford is built on steep wooded river banks near the confluence of the Frome and Avon. The medieval bridge affords the best viewpoint. The 19th-c. church up on the hill is of little interest, but opposite stands *Ivythorpe*, an early Georgian house with an elegant frontage. The part-Victorian *Old Brewery* is NE of the church down the hill; to the SE is *Old House*, another Georgian building. On the corner near the bridge is *The Inn*, with mullioned windows, dating from 1713.

Frome
3B

Somerset. Pop 13,800. 15m S of Bath (A361). Events: Cheese Show (3rd week Sep), Carnival (3rd Sat Sep). EC Thur MD Wed. Inf: Tel (0749) 73026

Frome (pronounced Froom) takes its name from the River Frome which flows under the main street. There was a settlement here in the 7th c., when St Aldhelm, Bishop of Malmesbury, built a church and monastery beside the local spring. Originally an agricultural town,

Frome developed a flourishing cloth industry during the 18th c. With its many hillside levels and steep streets, the town offers an interesting walking tour.

Start in the Market Place at the bridge (first built in 1667 and repaired several times since). Facing into town, on the left stands *The Blue House*, founded in 1726 as an almshouse for elderly women and a charity school. In the niche over the door can be seen the figure of an old lady and on either side of the door, two statues known as Nancy Guy and Billy Ball. Continuing into the Market Place, there are several fine Georgian façades to be seen, notably *The Crown Inn* and *The George Hotel* on the right. Turning left halfway up the hill, the pedestrian Cheap Street has several medieval timber-framed houses, and a water conduit runs down the middle of the street. At the top, turn left into King Street: the alley leading off on the left is also medieval.

Follow the ancient church wall round to the left until you come to the steps. These lead to an alleyway crossing the graveyard into St John's Forecourt. Pass through the arch into Bath Street. Uphill on the right can be seen a row of 17th- and 18th-c. stone cottages, while above them stands the *Rook Lane Congregational Chapel* (1707) – a fine example of a nonconformist chapel building.

Returning to the Forecourt, straight ahead is **St John's Church**, entered through a screen designed by Wyatville in 1814. The church dates from the 12th c. but was very heavily restored in the 19th c. At the E end stands the tomb of Bishop Ken (d. 1711) who was banished from the see of Bath and Wells for refusing to swear allegiance to William III. *The Blind House* in the SE corner of the churchyard is an old lock-up.

Out in the Forecourt again, turn left into the steep cobbled slope of Gentle Street. The first house on the right was built about 1760 for a dowager Duchess of Argyll. On the left stand *The Chantry* and *The Hermitage*, both part of a 17th-c. town house.

Glastonbury

Somerset. Town 5m SW of Wells (A39). Events:
Druid celebration of Beltane (May), Roman
Catholic pilgrimage (last Sun in May), Church of
England pilgrimage (last Sat in Jun), Glastonbury
Tor Fair (2nd week Sep). EC Wed MD Tue.
Inf: Tel (0458) 32954

Glastonbury's legendary name 'The Isle of Avalon' describes its original existence as an island rising out of surrounding marshland. The Iron Age lake villages (two of which have been identified to the NW of the town, built on piles) provide the earliest evidence of settlement in the area.

Since pre-Christian times, Glastonbury has been a focus for pilgrimage and mystical speculation. The legendary visit of Joseph of Arimathea in 30AD made it the spring of Christianity in these parts, and, it could be said, for the whole of Britain. Joseph, resting here on a missionary journey, planted his staff in the ground, at Weary-all Hill. Miraculously it sprouted into life, to become the famous 'Glastonbury Thorn'. This was seen by Joseph's disciples as a sign that their journey was over, and it was here that they built the first primitive church, to be replaced ultimately by the magnificent Glastonbury Abbey.

Most captivating of the legends surrounding Joseph concerns the Holy Grail, which, it is claimed, Joseph buried on Chalice Hill. Here the fabulous King Arthur, whose Knights pursued the sacred chalice, is drawn into the legend. Glastonbury is celebrated as the burial place of the king and his queen, Guinevere.

Glastonbury Abbey Approached through its gateway in Magdalene Street, near the Market Cross, the Abbey site includes the Abbey Church and monastic ruins, the Abbot's Kitchen and the Abbey grounds.

The ruins of the **Abbey Church** stand near the site of the original wattle-and-daub building of the primitive church. Successive churches were built here, and the Abbey's prestige grew with the appointment of St Dunstan (later Archbishop of Canterbury) as Abbot. St Dunstan's patron was King Edgar (d. 975) who was buried in the Abbey. By the time of the Domesday Book, Glas-

tonbury owned one-eighth of the entire modern county of Somerset.

The present building, started in 1184 and completed in the 16th c., was broken up after the Dissolution. The vestiges of the great church that remain give an idea of its vast size – at 563ft, longer than almost any medieval church in Europe. It was built in a combination of Romanesque and Gothic styles, spanning the three centuries of its construction. The first part of the building seen by visitors – and the most intact – is the *Lady Chapel*, standing at the W end of the church. This beautiful Norman building with well-preserved ornamental stonework (note the particularly fine N door) is one of Britain's finest Romanesque monuments. Within the chapel are a crypt, incorporating the Chapel of St Joseph, and St Joseph's Well.

The surviving parts of the church itself, though ruinous, are impressive and include the W door, part of the S wall of the nave, the NE and SE piers of the crossing, which supported the massive central tower, and parts of the choir and a N transept chapel. A marker in the choir shows the site of King Arthur's Tomb, another the chapel of King Edgar at the E end of the sanctuary.

To the S of the church the ground plans of the vanished abbey buildings are shown. To the SW is the **Abbot's Kitchen**, which contains an exhibition of the history of the Abbey. This octagonal building is one of the best-preserved medieval kitchens in Europe. From the fireplaces at the four corners, smoke was carried up the chimneys to the lantern in the roof. Unlike its fellow buildings it was not demolished to provide building materials after the Dissolution. Instead, it served first as a weavers' workshop, then as a Quaker meeting house, and during the 18th and 19th c. as a 'romantic ruin'.

To the N of the church is *St Patrick's Chapel*, dedicated to the apostle of Ireland who was associated with Glastonbury, and the *Abbey Museum*, which in addition to Abbey relics contains a scale model of the medieval buildings.

Leaving the Abbey precincts, turn

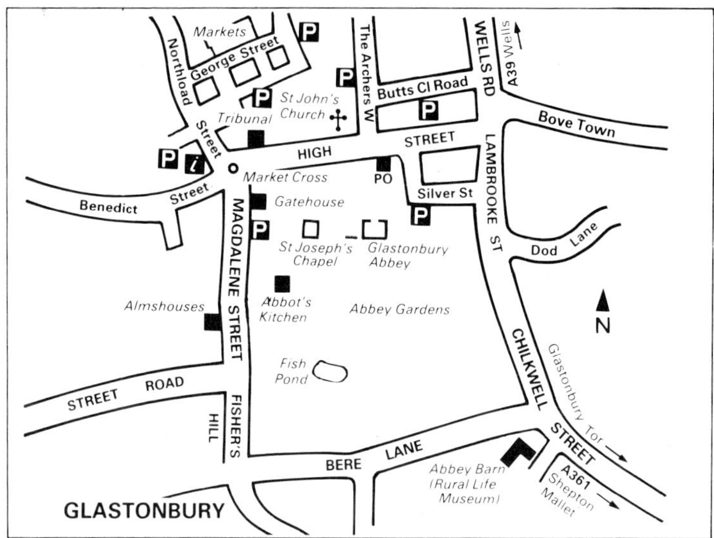

left down Magdalene Street. Shortly opposite are the 18th-c. *Pump House* (now private) built for visitors 'taking the waters' at Chalice Well, and the 16th-c. *Almshouses*, built in the precincts of a medieval hall hospital. *St Margaret's Chapel* (1270) which belonged to the hospital, has been recently restored.

Returning to Market Cross turn right into the High Street. On the left is the splendid 15th-c. Pilgrim's Inn, now known as *The George and Pilgrim's Hotel* (see p.15). One of the few remaining medieval inns in the country, the building has a central archway and the three-storey bays on either side have mullioned windows. Further up on the left the 15th-c. **Tribunal**, once the Abbey courthouse, is now a museum containing lake village finds, including the bronze Glastonbury bowl. Beyond stands Glastonbury's principal parish church, **St John the Baptist**, built on Norman foundations in the 15th c. Somerset is famous for its church towers, and St John's is an outstanding example of its period. 134ft high, it is the second tallest of Somerset parish church towers, with a delicate crown surmounted by battlements and pinnacles. The church's treasures include a 13th-c. ivory crucifix, the 15th-c. tombs of the church's benefactors – Richard and Joan Atwell – on either side of the sanctuary, and a 15th-c. Italian marble relief of the Nativity. In front of the church stands a splendid Glastonbury Thorn.

Glastonbury Tor Walk It is a stiff climb up the Tor, but the panoramic views of the surrounding plain, known as the Somerset Levels, from the top are worth the effort. From the High Street turn right down Lambrook and Chilkwell Street, passing the *Somerset Rural Life Museum*. The museum is housed in the 14th-c. **Abbey Barn**, with a magnificent wooden roof; inside there are exhibitions of crafts, cider-making, peat-digging and a wheelwright's shop. Continuing down Chilkwell Street, turn left into Wellhouse Lane and enter the *Chalice Well Gardens*; according to legend, the Holy Grail is said to have been buried here. The well once supplied the Abbey's water. From the gardens, cross to the opposite corner and follow the footpath up the slope.

The **Tor** (NT) stands on a major ley line in alignment with Stonehenge and the site of Canterbury Cathedral. (Ley lines are alignments between sites of mystical importance – churches, earthworks, stone circles – thought to have been used as guidelines for travellers or as invisible religious 'power paths'.) Although it looks man-made, excavations have shown the Tor to be a natural hill. Many theories have been advanced concerning its significance – as an ancient burial ground, as a 3000-year-old religious maze, or as a Celtic initiation centre. The area is even believed by some to stand within a configuration of the 12 signs of the Zodiac mapped out on the ground within a 30-mile circumference.

The tower crowning the Tor is all that remains of the 13th-c. Church of St Michael. From here, the Tor and the Abbey estate below can be seen to form a group of islands in a plain. Before it was drained, this plain was marshland, and Glastonbury, the legendary Avalon, was known as 'the isle of apples' or 'the isle of the blessed.'

Great Badminton   1C

Avon. Village off A46, 14m NE of Bath. Event: Badminton Horse Trials (Apr)

A traditional ducal village, Great Badminton (together with Badminton House) forms part of the Duke of Beaufort's estate. But of course Badminton has other associations: to the sporting world it is a magical name conjuring up the excitement of the annual four-day event: the Badminton Horse Trials.

The village has pleasant, wide streets of 18th and 19th-c. houses, including a pedimented terrace built about 1714 to house the Duke's ageing and retired retainers. There are also several 'Gothick' cottages built in utterly fantastic forms, such as ruined castles and log cabins. These, together with the late 18th-c. neo-classical **St Michael's Church** (attached to Badminton House) were designed by Thomas Wright. The church is a simple rectangular shape, with 18th-c. box pews and pulpits; its chancel and apse date from 1875. There are many memorials to the Beaufort family.

Badminton House, the heart of the Beaufort estate, is hardly visible from the village. Henry Somerset, Lord Herbert, was created Duke of Beaufort in 1682, in recognition of his noble descent from Edward III. The oldest part of Badminton House was built by the 1st Duke: later on (1740) the 3rd Duke commissioned William Kent to complete the house. Kent's work may be seen in the pavilions, cupolas and pediment on the central block, as well as Worcester Lodge in the park (the Lodge was later altered by Capability Brown). The interior has work by Grinling Gibbons and Wyatville. (Not open to the public.)

Great Chalfield Manor (NT)   2C/3C

Wilts. Historic house and church off B3107, 9m E of Bath

Set among water meadows, the moated late-medieval **Manor House** has known few changes since it was first built by Thomas Tropenell in 1467. One of the few surviving manor houses of the 15th c., the property includes the house, farm buildings and parish church, surrounded by a narrow moat. It was restored, and a S wing added, in the early 20th c.

Approached from the N over the moat and through a massive gatehouse into the forecourt, the front of the manor is asymmetrical, with yellow-grey stone walls and oriel windows. The impressive *Great Hall* is two storeys high with a garret above, lit from the gable ends; the ceiling has moulded beams with bosses. A screen at one end separates it from the adjoining kitchen and other rooms. Three spyholes in the walls are concealed behind hollow stone masks – so that occupants of the upper rooms could watch what was going on downstairs.

All Saints' Church, reached via the gatehouse, is 13th-c. Thomas Tropenell added the bell turret and spire, the S chapel and the stone screen. The panelled barrel roof and Perpendicular nave arch came later, while the three-decker pulpit, communion rails and chandelier are 17th-c. NE of the church are the remains of a summer house. Further E, the moat joins a fish pond.

Heytesbury 4C
Wilts. Village on A36, 2m SE of Warminster

Approaching the village from Warminster, a distinctive group of 18th-c. *Malthouses* stands out on the right. Beyond is the **Church of St Peter and St Paul**. Its tower is 13th-c., and its chancel has three 13th-c. pillars. The 15th-c. aisled nave has clerestory windows. The remainder of the building was restored in the 19th c. The stone screen in the Hungerford Chapel is exquisitely fanvaulted; three sickles – the mark of the Hungerford family – can be seen carved over the archway. Near the screen is the 17th-c. tomb of Thomas More and his wife with three kneeling alabaster figures. William Cunninton, the Wiltshire archaeologist, lies buried in the churchyard. Behind the church stands a Jacobean farmhouse.

Further along the road to the left is the tiny octagonal village *lock-up* and nearby, a block of 17th-c. almshouses known as the *Hospital of St John*; they were rebuilt in the original style after a fire in 1770. Beyond, on the right, is *The Angel* inn, with 17th-c. tea rooms. Finally, on the left, the late-18th-c. façade of *Heytesbury House* can be glimpsed through a gateway. This was the home for many years of the poet Siegfried Sassoon, and T.E. Lawrence used to visit the house when he was stationed at Bovington Camp.

Hinton Priory 3B
Avon. Medieval ruins off A36, 6m S of Bath

Hinton Priory was the second Carthusian monastery to be established in the country. It was founded in 1229 by Ela, Countess of Salisbury, in memory of her husband William Longespee, brother of Richard I. On the same day she attended the consecration of * *Lacock Abbey* in Wiltshire.

The well-preserved monastic ruins include the *Refectory Undercroft*; the *Chapter House* and above it the *Library*; the *Sacristy*; two dovecotes; parts of the *Guest House*; and the outlines of a *Church* and a *Great Cloister* surrounded by 14 individual small houses, each in a walled garden. After the Dissolution, in 1539, the local Hungerford family built the present, late 16th-c. *Manor House* (Hinton House) incorporating the Priory *Gatehouse* and *Porter's Lodge*.

Hinton Priory's most famous inmate was Nicholas Hopkins. While acting as spiritual director to the 3rd Duke of Buckingham, he predicted that Buckingham would succeed to the Throne – with the result that in 1521 Hopkins was imprisoned in the Tower of London and Buckingham executed. The incident is immortalised in Shakespeare's play *Henry VIII*.

Holt 3C
Wilts. Village and gardens on B3107, 11m E of Bath

The village, which once had its own spa, has little to interest the visitor – although there are some attractive 17th-c., Georgian and Victorian houses surrounding the green. But 1¼m NE is **The Courts** (NT), an early 18th-c. house whose beautiful grounds are open to the public. The gardens include interesting topiary, an arboretum and a delightful lily pond, with a neo-Georgian greenhouse (c.1900).

Horton Court (NT) 1B
Avon. Historic house and church off A46, 13m N of Bath

This restored medieval manor house of Cotswold stone stands with its church on a hillside beyond the village of Horton; above is an Iron Age hill fort.

Agnes and Hubert de la Rye gave the property to the Cathedral at Salisbury in 1125. Throughout the Middle Ages the house was occupied by a number of distinguished clergy, among them Archbishops of Canterbury and York. The oldest part of the building is a Norman hall (*c*.1140). The rest of the house displays the Italian taste favoured by William Knight, who was Prebendary of Horton from 1517 until 1541 when he became Bishop of Bath and Wells. The splendid front door has a Renaissance frieze and pilasters, while the late-Perpendicular ambulatory is embellished with four-centred arches and the stucco heads of Roman emperors.

The **Church of St James the Elder** next door is essentially 14th-c. Its most distinctive Perpendicular detail is the two-storeyed porch with a vaulted roof and carved capitals – one depicting a man playing pipes. The original Norman font was altered to an octagonal shape during the 17th c. Throughout the building there are memorials to the Paston family, who moved to Horton Court at the beginning of the 17th c.

Kelston 2B
Avon. Village on A431, 3m NW of Bath

Kelston was once part of a property belonging to the nunnery of Shaftesbury. After the Dissolution the estate was given to Audrey Malte – thought to have been a daughter of Henry VIII – on her marriage to John Harington. The Haringtons' house formerly stood on the site of what is now *Tower House*, an Italianate villa (*c*.1850). *Kelston Park* was built by John Wood the Younger, *c*.1770; the house has a terrace and fine view down the wooded slope to the River Avon below.

St Nicholas' Church has a broad, 13th-c. W tower with diagonal buttresses; the remainder of the building was heavily restored *c*.1860. There is some much-restored 14th- and 15th-c. stained glass work. W of the church stands *Manor Farm*, with a seven-bay barn and a dovecote said to have more nesting-holes than any other in the country. The picturesque *Crown Inn* has flagstone floors and old settles.

Kelston Round Hill, 2m to the NW, is worth the walk for the view it gives over to the Bristol Channel and, on a clear day, as far as the Black Mountains of Wales.

Kennet and Avon Canal
One of the West Country's most important industrial legacies from the 19th c. Designed by John Rennie and opened in 1810, the canal ranks alongside the Grand Union and the Leeds and Liverpool as an engineering masterpiece. The canal runs for 75m between Reading and Bath through some of the finest scenery in S and SW England, bisecting Wiltshire from E to W and linking the River Thames with the River Avon at Bath. Outside Devizes it passes through a spectacular flight of 29 locks over a 2m distance. Further W it travels over the picturesque Avoncliff and Dundas aqueducts, both designed by Rennie. At Claverton Pumping Station water is raised from the Avon to the canal using an ingenious system of waterwheels and beam-pumps.

The canal, which declined with the coming of the Great Western Railway in 1840, is now undergoing restoration by the Kennet and Avon Trust; it is expected to be entirely navigable by the late 1980s.

For details of boat trips and canal walks in the Bath area, see ps. 16-18.

Knap Hill
See *Alton Barnes*

Lacock (NT) 2C
Wilts. Village on A350. 3m S of Chippenham.
Event: Village Fair (Aug)

This old wool village, the property of the National Trust, is one of the most beautiful in England. Restored and carefully preserved, it looks much as it must have done two centuries ago. (No building is later than *c*. 1800.)

The village forms part of the manor of Lacock, which was granted to the Longespee family after the Norman Conquest. Some of its half-timbered, whitewashed houses and greystone cottages date back to the 14th c. The old buildings cover most aspects of traditional village life: there is a 14th-c. tithe barn, a drying loft, a tan factory, an old lock-up, a school – and on the outskirts, a pack horse bridge and ford.

St Cyriac's Church, standing on the W edge of the village, is a mainly 15th-c. building, with a lofty nave and a traceried window above the chancel arch. But its greatest beauty is the Lady Chapel, whose fan-vaulted roof, arches and slender columns are all exquisitely decorated. Sir William Sharington, who bought Lacock Abbey in 1540 after its dissolution, lies within the chapel in an elaborately carved tomb.

The **Fox Talbot Museum**, housed in a converted barn, stands at the gates of Lacock Abbey. It was at Lacock, in the 1830s, that William Henry Fox Talbot developed photography as we know it through his calotype process – a method of duplicating photographs in print form. His first successful photograph can be seen hanging in the S Gallery of the Abbey. The museum includes some of his early cameras and calotypes, together with a number of the awards made to him.

Lacock Abbey was founded in 1229 by Ela, Countess of Salisbury, who was Abbess here for 17 years. She established the Abbey and the Priory at Hinton Charterhouse, Somerset, on the same day, in memory of her husband William Longespee, a powerful baron and the illegitimate son of Henry II. While *Hinton Priory was designed to be a religious house for men, Lacock Abbey offered a religious finishing-school education to rich women, as well as helping the needy.

The Abbey has retained many of its original features: the cloisters (rebuilt in the 15th c.), kitchen, chapter-house and sacristy – even the warming room with its cauldron of bell-metal. However, the exterior reflects the changes of succeeding centuries in three distinct architectural phases: medieval, Renaissance and 18th-c. 'Gothick'.

When William Sharington bought the Abbey in the 16th c. he commissioned the stonemason John Chapman to make the building more comfortable and fashionable in the French and Italian Renaissance styles. The stable court, brewery, Stone Gallery, Blue Parlour and tower all date from this period. Inside the tower is Chapman's masterpiece – a remarkable stone table bearing the family's scorpion crest.

Two centuries later, Lacock's owner, John Ivory Talbot, updated the Abbey and its grounds – first in the Georgian, then in the 'Gothick' style. The *Great Hall* is an outstandingly original example of this idiosyncratic style, with its 'antiques', terracotta figures in niches, pointed-arch doorways and fireplace, and its ceiling emblazoned with the arms of Talbot's noble friends. So too is the broad carriage sweep leading up to the Abbey through an archway, and the picturesque W Front with its double flight of steps. Smooth parkland replaced the earlier, more formal gardens, and a ha-ha was made in front of the building. The many rare trees dotted across the park were planted by William Henry Fox Talbot in the 19th c.

Both Abbey and village were given to the National Trust by Miss Matilda Talbot in 1944.

Larkhall 2B (Bath area)
NE suburb of Bath off A4

St Saviour's Church (1829-32), built to the designs of John Pinch I, is in the early Gothic Revival style, similar to St Mary's, Bathwick. The interior has a gallery on three sides and a three-decker pulpit. The short chancel was added in 1882.

Limpley Stoke 3B
Wilts. Village off A36, 5m SE of Bath

Built on a steep hillside, Limpley Stoke runs into Freshford at its highest level and extends to the banks of the Avon at its lowest. At the top of the village is **St Mary's Church**, with a short W tower and some early features. The N porch entrance is early 13th c., and the aisle arcade incorporates the stonework of a narrow Saxon doorway, dating back to the 11th or even 10th c.

The Rose and Crown inn has a spectacular view of the valley and the **Dundas Aqueduct** which carries the Kennet and Avon Canal across the river; the aqueduct was designed by John Rennie *c.* 1805. Further down the hill by *The Hop Pole* inn there is a late 18th-c. weir. (See also *Walks 4 & 6*, p.18)

Little Sodbury Manor 1B
Avon. Historic house off A46, 11m N of Bath

This Cotswold manor house, set on a hill topped by a Roman camp site near the village of Little Sodbury, may be viewed by appointment only. Its outstanding feature is the *Great Hall*, first built *c.*1430, but with later Tudor, Jacobean and Queen Anne additions. The Hall contains a spyhole set behind a gargoyle.

The Manor is associated with the Wars of the Roses: in May 1471 Margaret of Anjou made a feint to Little Sodbury while trying to join the Lancastrian forces; Edward IV, leading the Yorkist army, is believed to have stayed overnight on the Roman camp site before marching along the top of the escarpment and intercepting her at Tewkesbury. The house also has links with William Tyndale, the translator of the Bible, who served as tutor to the children of Sir John Walsh, one of the house's owners. Sir John is known to have entertained Henry VIII and Anne Boleyn here. The gardens were created in the 1920s.

Little Solsbury Hill (NT)   2B
Avon. Ancient site off A4, 3m NE of Bath

The isolated hilltop of Solsbury commands a scenic view of Bath and its surrounding villages. The crown of the hill is marked by traces of an Iron Age camp whose builders probably knew and used the Bath springs. (see *Walk 5*, p.17)

Longleat   4C
Wilts. Historic house off A362, 4m SW of Warminster

An azalea drive leads to the Wiltshire home of the Marquess of Bath. In 1540 the estate, originally an Augustinian priory, was purchased by Sir John Thynne, later Elizabeth I's Lord High Treasurer. Thynne, an ancestor of the present Marquess of Bath, spent the rest of his life building the great house, overcoming such disasters as its near-destruction by fire in 1567. The architect he employed subsequent to this, Robert Smythson, was responsible for the fine symmetrical fronts of Bath stone. Sir Jeffrey Wyatville made alterations to the house in 1800-11, including the rebuilding of the N front. In the 1870s the 4th Marquess redesigned the State Rooms in the Italian Renaissance style. The park and the formal gardens next to the house were laid out by Capability Brown (1757-62) and later by Humphrey Repton.

Ground floor With most of the rooms refurbished in the Victorian period, the only room to retain its original appearance is the *Great Hall* (1559) with its stone-flagged floor and hammerbeam roof. The minstrels' gallery, carved screen and fireplace are slightly later (*c.* 1600) as is the small balcony (*c.* 1666) at the opposite end of the hall to the gallery. Displayed on the minstrels' gallery are the arms of Sir John Thynne, his parents, two wives and children. The central shield on top is that of the Protector Somerset, who ruled for the boy king Edward VI (1547-52). It was Somerset who knighted Thynne during the Battle of Pinkie against the Scots. (A Scottish lion with a twisted tail was subsequently incorporated in the Thynne coat of arms.) The Hall's contents include a 33ft-long oak table *c.* 1600, an unusual English wall-clock *c.* 1620, a late 18th-c. 24-hr astronomical clock, and the antlers of a prehistoric Irish elk. The series of hunting scenes is by John Wootton (*c.* 1740).

The house's other rooms are much later. The *Lower East Corridor*, with its 16th-c. Brussels tapestries, is the work of Wyatville, and the *Ante-Library* was one of seven rooms elaborately redecorated in the Italian style by Crace & Co (1870s).

The *Red Library* houses 6000 of the 30,000 volumes making up the Longleat Collection, one of the finest private libraries in the world. Most of the collection is not on public view. Apart from its books, the Red Library is interesting for its magnificent Wedgwood-style ceiling, *c.* 1878, with cameo-like panel paintings. A portrait of Bishop Ken, one-time Bishop of Bath and Wells, who spent the last twenty years of his life at Longleat with his friend Viscount Weymouth, hangs on the left just inside the library entrance. Other rooms on the ground floor are the *Breakfast Room* and *Lower Dining Room*, with ornate ceilings modelled on originals in the Ducal Palace, Venice. Both rooms contain an array of family portraits.

First floor The *Bath Bedroom* contains the first bath to be installed in the house (1840). The three State Rooms, where Elizabeth I was the first monarch to be entertained, in 1574, are particularly fine. The *State Dining Room* has walls of tooled Spanish leather with portraits of the Thynne family. The ceiling, *c.* 1860, frames pictures from the School of Titian. Some exceptionally fine pieces of silver and snuff-boxes are on display. The 90-ft *Saloon* is the longest room in the house, with a ceiling inspired by one in the Palazzo Massima in Rome, c. 1875. 16th-c. French and Flemish tapestries adorn the walls, while the hooded fireplace is copied from one in the Doge's Palace in Venice. The *State Drawing Room* is more Italianate still. The ornate ceiling is adapted from one in the library of St Mark's Cathedral, Venice, and Genoese velvet, *c.* 1650, covers the walls. The paintings, by early Italian Masters, were collected by the 4th Marquess; the central picture in the 'Holy Family' group is attributed to Titian.

The Thynne family's Coronation robes are on display in the *Dress Corridor*; their State Coach can be seen at the foot of the *Grand Staircase*. The staircase itself and the well were designed by Wyatville.

Among the estate's other attractions are the Victorian kitchens, Lord Weymouth's erotic murals, a collection of 19th-c. dolls' houses, and various exhibitions in the outbuildings, as well as a Garden Centre. A maze, fun fair and train rides make this a perfect family outing.

The principal draw, however, is still Longleat's **Safari Park** – the first in Europe. Hundreds of wild animals roam freely here, including elephants, rhinos, monkeys and the famous 'Lions of Longleat'. On one of the reserves visitors may leave their cars and wander among the zebras and giraffes, or take a boat ride to Gorilla Island. An attractive walk near Longleat is *Heaven's Gate*, which follows a ½m. route through woodlands to a splendid view overlooking the estate.

Marlborough 2D

Wilts. Town on A4, 32m NE of Bath. EC Wed MD Wed, Sat. Inf: Tel (0380) 4911

Marlborough lies in the Kennet valley surrounded by the Downs and Savernake Forest. The town once occupied an important position on the stagecoach route from London to Bath. Now it is the commercial focus for a wide area of Wiltshire and the home of a famous public school.

At the NE end of the broad High Street stands **St Mary's**, a Norman church rebuilt in the 17th c.; a Norman doorway can be seen under the W tower. The battlements above the S porch are 15th-c.; the stone cat alongside them commemorates a courageous cat said to have rescued its kittens from the blazing building during a fire in the Middle Ages. Some fragments of Roman sculpture have been let into the church wall, among them a carving of the goddess Fortuna. A curfew bell is rung each evening. A flagged path leads from the church to *The Green*, surrounded by Georgian houses. In front of St Mary's stands the *Town Hall*, built in 1901 in the style of the late 17th-c.

The **High Street** itself is one of the most beautiful in the country. It has many fine Georgian buildings, and on the N side, several of the shops are colonnaded. Picturesque passages and alleys lead off the street, and in them can be seen a few timbered buildings which survived the town's great fire of 1653. The High Street's most notable building is *The Castle and Ball* inn, halfway along. Largely rebuilt in the 18th c., the inn was a fashionable halt for coaches on their way to Bath (see also p.15). Among the other elegant Georgian buildings are *The Ivy House Hotel* and *The Georgian Restaurant*. At the SW end of the High Street on the corner of Hyde Lane stands *The Sun* inn, a medieval building with 19th-c. additions. Inside, many of its ancient features have survived: panelling, timbers, and a doorway leading down to the cellars. Also at this end of the street, on an island, stands the **Church of St**

Peter and St Paul, where Thomas Wolsey was ordained as a priest in 1498. Its magnificent tower is 120 ft high. Inside, the porch and chancel are vaulted, and there is a finely carved reredos and arches decorated with angels.

The W end of the town is dominated by the buildings of **Marlborough College**. The great, tree-covered prehistoric mound standing in the school grounds (**Castle Mound**) may well have given the town its name, for 'marl' means 'chalky soil', while 'borough' means a mound or barrow. Stone Age and Roman remains have been found here, and a medieval castle once stood on the mound. Eventually, the castle was rebuilt as a mansion, and the mansion converted into an inn. It was during the 19th c. that the Reverend Charles Plater selected the building to be the nucleus of his new college for the sons of clergymen.

Among the College buildings lining the road is the *Chapel*. It contains a series of impressive murals painted by Spencer Stanhope, depicting a number of Biblical subjects; there is also a stained glass window by William Morris, who spent his schooldays at the College. A flight of steps leads from the Chapel to the columned *Hall* built in memory of Marlborough's Old Boys who died during the First World War.

1m SW of Marlborough (A4) is a *White Horse*, cut in the hillside in 1804.

Marshfield 2B
Avon. Town on A420, 7m N of Bath. Event: Boxing Day Mummers

During the 17th and 18th c. the town's prosperity was based on its wool and the malt it produced for both Bath and Bristol. The large malthouses still standing are a reminder of its past economy.

The picturesque High Street, once a busy coaching stop on the way to Bristol, has been quiet and unspoilt since the coming of the bypass. At one end stand the *Crispe Almshouses* (1619) and further along, *Tolzey Hall* (1690, rebuilt 1793). There are two Georgian inns, *The Crown* and *The Catherine Wheel*. At the other end of the street beyond Market Place stands the **Church of St Mary the Virgin**. Something of the building's Norman structure can be seen in the blocked arch on the S arcade; the rest of the church is Perpendicular.

The town is famous for its Marshfield Mummers. Each Boxing Day they produce a traditional mumming play, dressed in newspaper costumes.

Meare 4A
Somerset. Village on B3151, 8m SW of Wells

The village is named after the great lake – 5m in circumference – which was finally drained during the 18th c. The well-preserved *Iron Age lake village* excavated on the site of the marshland is thought to have been occupied in two phases – first by peasant farmers, later by metalworkers and weavers. Finds from the settlement, including some delicate basketwork, can be seen in the Tribunal museum at *Glastonbury*.

The *Manor House* forms part of the former summer palace set up by the Abbots of Glastonbury *c.* 1340. Originally it was an L-shaped building with the Hall located E of the entrance, while the back wing housed a 60ft-long upper room. Across a field to the E stands the 14th-c. *Fish House*, used for salting and stoning fish for the Glastonbury monks. The two-storeyed building with its outside staircase is open to view at any time.

St Mary's Church was also in the keeping of the Abbots. The chancel and W tower were set up in 1323; of the 14th-c. additions, the S door has distinctive ornate ironwork. Abbot Selwood added the nave in the 15th c.

Melksham 2C
Wilts. Town on A365, 12m E of Bath. Event: Carnival (Aug)

After Swindon, Melksham is the most industrialised town in the county, with Avon Tyres its largest manufacturer. From the Market Place, Church Street leads down to Canon Square, with its pleasant cluster of 17th-c. and early 18th-c. houses, and the picturesque lanes down Church Walk. The school standing nearby was originally a buttressed tithe barn.

St Michael's Church is a large Perpendicular building with traces of Norman and 13th-c. work; its interior was substantially altered by T.H. Wyatt in the 1840s. There are several memorials: one is to an entire Melksham family who died at sea on the *Titanic*.

Mells
3B

Somerset. Village off A362, 3m NW of Frome

The village reflects its rich medieval past when, as a clothmaking centre, it belonged to Glastonbury Abbey.

The nursery rhyme 'Little Jack Horner' first originated in Mells. At the time of the Dissolution — so the story goes – the Abbot of Glastonbury sent his steward, Jack Horner, to present a bribe to Thomas Cromwell, in the hope of keeping the Abbey intact. The bribe consisted of a pie containing the title deeds of twelve of the Abbey's manorial properties. On his way Jack Horner is said to have lifted up the pie-crust and removed for himself the deed of Mells. The part-Tudor, gabled and mullioned *Mells Manor* was the home of the Horner family until the early 20th century. It was then that Katherine Horner married Raymond Asquith, son of the British prime minister Herbert Asquith: their descendants, the present Lord and Lady Asquith, still live here.

St Andrew's Church, approached through an avenue of yews, is an outstanding example of the Somerset Perpendicular style, with pinnacles, battlements and gargoyles. The 104ft tower has blind tracery, pierced stone windows and pinnacled buttresses up to the parapet. Inside, a splendid fanvaulted roof rests on a dozen stone angels. The church has some interesting memorials. Raymond Asquith's has an inscription engraved by Eric Gill. A memorial to Laura Lyttelton, wife of the politician Alfred Lyttelton, takes the form of a peacock; the design is by Edward Burne-Jones. The Horner Chapel contains a bronze horse and rider representing Edward Horner; the statue is by Alfred Munnings and the pedestal by Lutyens. The St Francis of Assisi window is by William Nicholson.

The Mendips
3A

One of Somerset's loveliest natural areas: a region of limestone ridges and valleys between Burrington in the W and West Cranmore in the E. What local people refer to as 'Mendip' is the bleak plateau on top of the hills. The name is a combination of two Celtic words meaning 'hill' and 'valley'. See also *Cheddar* (Gorge and Caves), *Wookey Hole* (Caves) *Priddy* and *Burrington Combe*.

Midsomer Norton
3B

Avon. Town on A362, 9m SW of Bath

This town was built around the industry it shared with neighbouring Radstock– coal. Its picturesque name comes partly from the Saxon meaning 'north town', while the later addition 'Mid-somer' is taken from the annual mid-summer fair once held to commemorate the Eve of St John – the town's patron saint.

The original village is still evident in the older houses around the church on the hill. Of the original 17th-c. **Church of St John Baptist**, only the tower remains, with a statue of Charles II in a niche; the rest was restored in 1830, and the chancel and Lady Chapel rebuilt in the 20th c. Under a tree in the churchyard can be seen a memorial to a coal-pit disaster in 1859; twelve men and boys are buried there – the youngest only twelve years old. The Roman Catholic **Church of the Holy Ghost** is the town's oldest building. Created from a 15th-c. barn, it was designed by Sir Giles Gilbert Scott and consecrated in 1913. The fine work inside reflects Downside Abbey's great interest in the parish.

Milk Hill

See *Alton Barnes*

Norton St Philip
3B

Somerset. Village on A366, 9m S of Bath

A famous hostelry here is *The George Inn* – one of the finest surviving medieval inns in the country. What is more, travellers can still enjoy a good lunch – just as Samuel Pepys did in 1668 when, as his diary recounts, his household 'dined very well' for 10 shillings. Built in the 15th c. by the monks of nearby Hinton Priory, the brownstone inn has an arched entrance and a flight of outside steps leading to the half-timbered floors above. This was probably used as a loading platform for waggons carrying cloth or wool: the monks, who were sheep farmers, used their hospice as a storehouse for wool. (See also p.15.)

Nunney 4B
Somerset. Village off A361, 3m SW of Frome

Nunney has Somerset's finest castle, best seen on the approach from Frome. The moated **Nunney Castle** dates from 1372 onwards, when Sir John De la Mare (later Sheriff of Somerset) received licence 'to fortify and crenellate his manse at Nunney'. The castle is rectangular with a four-storey keep and four round turreted towers placed symmetrically at each corner. The terrace was added later. Inside, three upper floors were built above the kitchens; the fireplace and oven are still visible. A staircase in the NE tower leads to the Great Hall on the second floor; above it were the solar and possibly a guardroom. The chapel stood in the SW tower. Lighting was by slits only.

The castle remained intact until the Civil War. In 1645 the N wall was breached after its owner, Colonel Richard Prater, a Royalist, was besieged by Roundhead forces. Afterwards the structure decayed and in 1910 the N wall and entrance front caved in.

NW of the castle stands *Manor House Farm*, a two-storeyed house with five bays dating from the early 18th c. The rest of the village consists of 17th and 18th-c. stone houses and earlier thatched cottages clustered around a stream and the High Street, where *The George Inn* stands. **All Saints' Church** is probably Saxon in origin; a fragment of a Saxon cross is set into the N wall of the chancel. The spiral fluted font is Norman. The S porch, the tower, the nave with its barrel roof and the wooden chancel screen were all built *c.* 1525; the 13th-c. chancel was restored during the 19th c. There are a number of effigies in the N transept, including those of Sir John De la Mare, Sir John Poulet and his wife Constance, and Richard Prater and his wife – all past owners of the castle.

Oakhill Manor 3B
Somerset. Country house and museum off A367, 14m SW of Bath

The manor house, just outside Oakhill village, houses a **Model Transport Museum**, with models and pictures relating to land, sea, air and military transport. The collection includes some of the world's finest models – among them an 'N' gauge electric indoor railway. Outside, there is a miniature railway, with a close-to-scale track, locomotives, rolling stock and stations.

Oldbury Castle
See *Cherhill*

Orchardleigh Park 3B
Somerset. Country house and church off A361 (Lullington), 2m N of Frome

The picturesque **house**, home of the Duckworth family, was designed in a mixture of Elizabethan styles by T.H. Wyatt during the 1850s. In the grounds stand an 18th-c. rotunda and, beside the lake, a Georgian boathouse. At the W end of the lake a bridge leads over to the island *Church of St Mary*. In the churchyard lies buried Sir Henry Newbolt (d. 1938), author of *Drake's Drum* and of the famous line 'Play up! Play up! and play the game'. The church probably dates from the 13th c.; there is some fine detail in the chancel and good 15th- and 16th-c. glass. A memorial tablet to Sir Henry Newbolt and his wife can be seen on the N wall. The church is ¼m walk from the house. The nearby village of *Lullington* has a Norman church with a splendid N door.

Overton Hill 2D
Wilts. Ancient site off A4, 5m W of Marlborough

Crossed by the A4, this is an area of prehistoric earthworks, ditches and tumuli, The most important site, across the river by the village of East Kennet, is

The Sanctuary, believed to have been a ritual centre. The site was excavated just before the Second World War and the missing sarsen stones replaced with concrete markers; there is little to be seen now apart from a few remaining sarsens. Excavations have shown that the sarsens (*c*. 2000-1600 BC) replaced wooden structures even older than the stone circles at nearby Avebury.

A line of stones known as *West Kennet Avenue* runs NW of Overton Hill towards Avebury. Originally the avenue ran for 1½m.

Two long barrows lie in the vicinity: to the S the *East Kennet Long Barrow*, to the W the *★West Kennet Long Barrow*.

Pewsey   3D
Wilts. Town on A345, 13m E of Devizes, 7m S of Marlborough

A statue of Alfred the Great (1911) marks the crossroads at the town centre. **St John Baptist's Church**, standing high above the main road, dates back to the 13th c.; its late Norman arcades are founded on huge sarsen stones. The chancel is early 14th-c., while the tower is Perpendicular. The S chapel, pulpit, lectern and stalls were added by G.E. Street in 1861. The wood-carving of the font cover and the reredos and the painted spandrels of the nave arcades are all the work of Canon Bertrand Play-dell-Bouverie, rector from 1880-1910.

Court House, a timber-framed and thatched building, stands between the church and the *Rural District Council Offices* (formerly the rectory, built *c*. 1700). At the E end of the High Street there is another timber-framed and thatched building, *Ball House*. The road W to Wilcot passes the old work-house (1836), now *Pewsey Hospital*.

1m SW of the town lies a pagan *Saxon cemetery*; excavations begun in 1969 have revealed 60 burials, both adults and children. On *Martinsell Hill*, 2½m NE of Pewsey, stands an Iron Age hill fort enclosing 32 acres. *Pewsey White Horse* can be seen on the side of the hill 1¼m S of the town in the Vale of Pewsey; first cut in 1785, the figure was re-cut to commemorate the coronation of George VI.

Potterne   3C/3D
Wilts. Village on A360, 2m S of Devizes

The village, set against a steep hill, was once the property of the Bishops of Salisbury. **Porch House**, in the High Street, is one of England's most famous late 15th-c. timber-framed houses. A hall house of the simplest type, with a hammerbeam roof, it was restored in 1876 for the painter George Richmond to live in. In the grounds, traces of a 10th-c. timber church were found.

St Mary's Church, set above the main street, is a classic Early English building – cruciform, with a broad pin-nacled and battlemented tower over the crossing. The porches were probably added later. Inside there is a tub-shaped Saxon font with a Latin inscription round the rim. Near the church gates stands *Church House*, dated 1614; it has symmetrical gables, a two-storeyed, gabled porch and mullioned windows.

Priddy   3A
Somerset. Village and ancient site off B3135, 6m NW of Wells. Event: Sheep Fair (Aug)

Set on the bleak heights of Mendip, the sprawling village is dominated by its church and by the ancient Nine Bar-rows. Potholers come from far and wide to explore the underground limestone caves in the area.

Four roads meet at the green; in the centre stands a thatched stack of sheep hurdles. The inhabitants believe that as long as this stack remains on the green they will be able to hold their 600-year-old Sheep Fair here.

St Lawrence's Church has a 13th-c. tower, although its later medieval his-tory is unclear. The oak screen in the chancel is Tudor and there is a fine barrel roof. To one side of the church, in a glass case on the wall, can be seen an exquisite 16th-c. altar frontal, executed in gold thread on damask.

Nine Barrows Lane leads up to *Prid-dy Nine Barrows* and the adjoining *Ashen Hill Barrows*. In 1815, archaeolo-gists excavating these 4000-year-old earthworks produced evidence of cre-mation burial; among their finds were a bronze weapon, a ring, a miniature pot-tery vessel and five amber beads almost identical to those found in the tombs of Egyptian mummies of the same period.

1½m NE of the village, *Priddy Circles* consist of four large earthen rings, each 550ft across, set side by side; their exact age and purpose are not known. The track of a Roman road passes between them.

Prior Park
2B (Bath area)

Avon. Historic house off A3062, 1m S of Bath

The steps of Prior Park command the most celebrated view of the city of Bath. The impressive house was built by stonemerchant and entrepreneur Ralph Allen for entertaining his friends and to show off the quality of the Bath stone produced in his quarries at Combe Down. Building started in 1734: the architect John Wood the Elder was commissioned to design a house on the grand scale in the then highly fashionable Palladian style.

The house is 15 bays wide with a large six-columned central portico looking N through the curved vale to Bath; it is connected to pavilions on the E and W by a splendid sweep of curved one-storeyed arcades. Originally, a 90-ft gallery ran the length of the building, but was destroyed in the fire of 1836.

The only part of the mansion to have survived virtually untouched since the 1740s is the *chapel* at the E end. Inside, the apse has a richly-coffered half dome and the walls have two tiers of columns and pilasters, Corinthian above and Ionic below. In the W wing is the later *College Chapel*, belonging to the Catholic boy's school which at present occupies the building. Designed as a church by J.J. Scoles in 1844 and completed in 1882 the chapel has an impressive classical interior, with the nave and aisles separated by eight fluted Corinthian columns. The chapel and four rooms are open to visitors.

In the grounds a fine Palladian Bridge (1755) based on designs at Stowe and Wilton, stands across the dam of an artificial water basin; it was probably built under the influence of Capability Brown, whom Allen employed to landscape the gardens.

When Allen died in 1764 the house passed through various hands. In 1817 a Benedictine monk, Bishop Baines, opened a Catholic boys' school and seminary to train priests. He made several alterations and employed the architect H.E. Goodridge to build a curved stairway in front of the portico, leading down the hillside. After the 1836 fire which destroyed much of the building, Baines refitted the interior of the house with purchases from the derelict Hunstrete House, nearby; these included a grand staircase, fire-places and panelling. (See also *Walk 3*, p.17)

Priston Mill
3B

Avon. Industrial site off A367, 6m SW of Bath

A signpost just past Priston village leads off to the site. This is a working corn mill, with a waterwheel which produces most of the stoneground flour and oats used in the area. The mill was first mentioned in the Domesday survey of *c.* 1087 when it was owned by the monastic church of Bath. The present building is about 200 years old. Earlier this century the equipment was used mainly as a water grist mill – that is, to grind corn for cattle feed. The recent increased demand for stoneground flour has brought the mill back into use.

Visitors can watch the milling process from start to finish. The mill shop sells bread, wholewheat flour, butter, cheese and local craft work.

Radstock
3B

Avon. Town on A367, 8m SW of Bath

With nearby Midsomer Norton, this town was associated with the region's now defunct coal industry, which operated from the mid-18th c. to 1973.

Rode
3C

Somerset. Aviary gardens off A36, 10m SE of Bath.

A left turning off the main road at *The Red Lion* pub, Woolverton, leads to **Rode Tropical Bird Gardens**. Rode Manor's 17 acres of woods and gardens provide the setting for the all-bird zoo. The collection includes over 180 species of birds, among them macaws, owls, mynah birds, flamingoes, ornamental pheasants and penguins – most of them uncaged. Water birds roost along the chain of small lakes in the grounds. Domestic animals such as tortoises and terrapins are kept at Pets Corner, and there is a souvenir gift shop.

Continuing into Rode village, in the High Street stands the *Min Lewis Pram and Toy Museum*.

St Catherine's Court 2B
Avon. Historic house off A4, 3m NE of Bath

St Catherine's is tucked away in a deep wooded valley which once belonged to Bath Abbey. It has associations with Henry VIII and Elizabeth I. The delightful Tudor house was enlarged from Prior Cantlow's late medieval priory grange by William Blanchard in the early 17th c.; the building was further enlarged in the 19th c. The N front has three symmetrical gables, a two-storeyed porch and mullioned windows. Inside, some of the rooms are panelled, with decorative carving. The house's great treasure is a portrait of *Catherine of Aragon* by the studio of Holbein. The Renaissance gardens descending in a series of terraces to the road were created *c.* 1600.

The tiny 15th-c. **St Catherine's Church** was built by Prior Cantlow to replace an earlier Norman building; a Norman font and a few Norman stones in the tower survive. In the nave is a beautiful St Catherine window, with the saint standing on a broken wheel. To the left of the altar stands the 17th-c. tomb of William Blanchard and his wife with their children.

Saltford 2B
Avon. Village on A4, 5m NW of Bath

Built along the River Avon, Saltford is the home of the local Yacht Club and of **Saltford Marina** – a new development catering for every taste, from high-speed motorboats to the more traditional narrowboat. *The Jolly Sailor* pub is only a short distance away. **St Mary's Church** has a 17th-c. tower with traces of its Norman origins; the font is probably 13th-c. while the pulpit is Jacobean. (See also *Walk 7*, p. 18.)

Saltford Manor, N of the church, is the oldest inhabited house in the county and one of the oldest in England. It has retained its original Norman ceiling beams and arch; the Hall, which was once on the upper floor, has now gone. Parts of the building are Tudor. The front is 17th-c. On the second floor have been found traces of a wall painting showing a seated Virgin and a Wheel of Fortune.

Scratchbury Camp 4C
Wilts. Ancient site off A36, 3m SE of Warminster

This late Iron Age hill fort, built *c.* 250 BC, towers over the village of Norton Bavant below. Its ramparts follow the shape of the hill around the summit, sometimes reaching 66ft in height. The camp centre contains traces of a bank and ditch which may well date from an earlier camp (*c.* 2000 BC). Within the ramparts are seven Bronze Age barrows. Nearby, in a 12ft-high, elongated Stone Age grave, archaeologists found wild boar teeth, pieces of stag-horn, charcoal and stones.

Sham Castle 2B (Bath area)
Avon. Folly off Bathwick Hill, 1m E of Bath

Ralph Allen, the Bath stonemerchant, had the folly built in 1762 so that he could see it on the skyline when he looked out from his town house. The battlemented folly, probably designed by Sanderson Miller, consists of two round towers joined with an arch and flanked by two smaller square towers. At night it is illuminated. (See also *Walk 2*, p. 17.)

Sheldon Manor 2C
Wilts. Historic house off A420, 2m W of Chippenham

Dating from 1282, this charming stone manor is well worth a visit. A remarkable survival of the original 13th-c. house is the unusual two-storey porch, seemingly too large for the building. Its ground floor has a stone-vaulted ceiling and an original stone water cistern fed by pipes leading from the roof. Parts of the house are 15th-c., but much is a rebuilding of *c.* 1660 with the mullioned windows and tall gables of the period.

Inside, there is a handsome oak staircase and a fine collection of furniture.

The stylised gardens include formal terraced rose beds, an orchard, a water garden and a 15th-c. chapel. Sheldon is well-known for its afternoon teas.

Shepton Mallet 4B
Somerset. Town 5m SE of Wells (A371). Events: Royal Bath and West Show (end May/early Jun), Mid-Somerset Agricultural Show (Aug), Cheese Show (Sep), Carnival (Nov). EC Wed MD Fri. Inf: Tel (0749) 73026

Up to the middle of the 19th c. the name Shepton Mallet was synonymous with the wool trade. 'Shepton' comes from a Saxon form of 'sheeptown', while 'Malet' is a Norman name. Nowadays the town is known for its shoes, gloves, cheese and above all, for Showering's 'Babycham' and cider factory in the NE part of the town.

The central Market Place is a pedestrian precinct. Its *Market Cross* was originally built *c.* 1500; the present near-reproduction cross stands 50ft high with a central spire, pinnacles, six arches and a stone-paved floor. A few yards away, under a narrow tiled roof, stand the oldest wooden *Shambles* in England; they were originally a meat market.

Isolated behind the new building development is the **Church of St Peter and St Paul**. Its tower is famous – probably the earliest of Somerset's Perpendicular towers, dramatically built with pinnacled buttresses and huge gargoyles. The church was founded in late Saxon or early Norman times (there are transitional Norman arcades dating from *c.* 1190, and even earlier walls); it was rebuilt in the 15th c. The wagon roof is made up of 350 carved oak panels. The plain, round font is Saxon, the pulpit 16th-c., cut from a single stone. Two 13th-c. stone knights (probably of the Malet family) can be seen, one in the E, one in the W window.

S of the church stand the 17th-c. *Strode Almshouses*, while on the other side is the building which originally housed the town's *Grammar School*, dating from the same period. Shepton Mallet's *Museum* stands in Town Street, S of the Market Place, with relics from the Hyaena's Den at Wookey Hole, as well as Roman pottery and coins, old views of the town and geological specimens. The *Unitarian Chapel* (1692) in Cowl Street, N of the Market Place, has a magnificent carved oak pulpit.

Shepton Mallet is a byword in the West of England for the four-day annual 'Bath & West' agricultural show. Its attractions include show jumping, field sports, shire horses, a motor fair, sheep dog trials, sheep shearing, traction engines, a stock section and sales of local produce.

4m SW of Shepton Mallet, off the A371, is North Wootton village and *Wootton Vines*. Visitors can walk around the vineyard and buy wine, cider and vines at the shop.

Silbury Hill 2D
Wilts. Ancient site off A4, 6m W of Marlborough

The largest man-made mound in Europe, Silbury covers 5¼ acres at its base and rises to 130ft; it was once even larger, but has eroded into its surrounding ditch. The earthwork has been carbon-dated to *c.* 2750 BC.

Several excavations have taken place between 1776 and 1969, but only boulders and stones have been found. According to legend, Silbury was constructed as a burial mound for a king called Sil – but more recent opinion has suggested that the mound may have been a gigantic sundial and measure for determining the seasons.

Silbury Hill is in the care of the Department of the Environment. It lies close to the A4, and can be seen from Avebury.

N of the hill stands the prehistoric stone circle of *★Avebury*, and beyond it the Neolithic earthworks of *★Windmill Hill*, while to the E lies *★West Kennet Long Barrow*.

South Stoke 3B
Avon. Village off A367, 2m S of Bath

Though close to Bath the village, set on a steep incline, is remarkably unspoilt. **St James's Church** has a Perpendicular W tower and pulpit; the N doorway is Norman. *Manor Farmhouse* dates back to the late 17th c., with a fine barn (*c.* 1500). *The Packhorse Inn*, with its gables and mullioned windows, is dated 1674; its special attractions are cider and shove ha'penny, and a garden.

Midford Castle, 1m E of the village off the B3110, is a fine example of the 18th-c. 'Gothick'. Built *c.* 1775 for Henry Disney Roebuck (possibly to a design by John Carter), the three-storeyed, castellated building is on a trefoil plan said to represent the ace of clubs, with a 19th-c. gatehouse and stables, a ruined chapel and a summer house in the garden.

South Wraxall 2C
Wilts. Village off B3109, 9m E of Bath

The building of greatest interest in this village is *South Wraxall Manor*, begun *c.* 1430. It is still owned by the family of the man who built it, Robert Long. Approached through a 15th-c. gatehouse, the house is built around three sides of a courtyard. The 15th-c. hall is the full height of the house. To the SW stands an octagonal summer house with a domed roof. *Manor Farmhouse* nearby was once a 14th-c. hospice; the Hall and Chapel of St Audoen still survive.

St James's Church has a tower dating back to *c.* 1300, with a saddle-back roof and a big stair turret. Inside, the building is heavily restored. The Long Chapel contains monuments ranging from a medieval tomb chest to a memorial commemorating the second Viscount Long, killed in action in Holland during the Second World War.

Stanton Drew 2A
Avon. Village and ancient site off B3130, 11m W of Bath

By the River Chew in the fields to the E of the village are Stanton Drew's **Stone Circles**, which form one of the finest prehistoric monuments in Wessex. The site, ½m across, consists of three circles with linking avenues, a single stone known as *Hauteville's Quoit*, two megalithic stones joinly known as *The Middle Ham*, and a stone near the church known as *The Cove* – possibly part of a chamber tomb.

27 of the original 30 stones remain. The whole complex, dating from the Bronze Age Beaker period (2000-1600 BC), is thought to have been designed to observe sunrise on Midsummer Day. *Hauteville's Quoit*, located across the river near the road, has a strange story attached to it. Sir John Hauteville is said to have rolled it down Maes Knoll to the N in a fit of temper after receiving Norton estate – which he considered a paltry reward – from King Edward I in recompense for military services. His misfortune is commemorated in the name of the nearby estate, Norton Malreward.

Stanton Drew itself has vestiges of its medieval past, including the part-Norman *St Mary's Church* (restored 1889), the vicarage and the bridge on the road to Chew Magna. There is a tithe barn in the village, and on the outskirts stands a curious little whitewashed and thatched building, its roof crowned with a game bird; it was formerly the toll-house.

Steeple Ashton 3C
Wilts. Village off A350, 4m E of Trowbridge

The name of this village recalls the steeple which once graced the splendid parish church whose tower is still a dominant feature of the plain. The outskirts of the village are dull, but the centre is pretty, with timbered and red-brick houses along the main street and a triangular village green. The octagonal *Lock-up* is set on the green with the *Village Cross* beside it. Nearby are the half-timbered *Post Office*, *Market House*, the gabled 17th-c. *Manor* and the *Vicarage*, a 14th-c. building with subsequent additions.

St Mary's Church, beyond the green, is a good example of the Perpendicular style, built 1480-1500. The interior is light and elaborately vaulted. Much of the glass is 15th-c. Set on the N wall is a palimpsest brass: one side holds a tribute to Deborah Marks, who died in 1730 at the age of 99 having seen the reigns of seven kings and queens; on the back is a satirical verse attacking Roman Catholicism, together with an unflattering image of Queen Anne.

Stockton   4C

Wilts. Village off A36, 8m SE of Warminster

Time has hardly touched this village. Its main street is lined with quaint half-timbered and thatched estate cottages. Approaching the village from the W, you see *Stockton House* on the left, set in its own wooded grounds. Built by John Topp, this is a fine Elizabethan building with triple gables. Above the house on the Down is the symbol of the *Australian Rising Sun*, cut into the hillside during the First World War by the Australian Commonwealth Military Forces.

On the left of the main street stands *The Carrier's Arms*, a picturesque inn with a fascinating history of the village above the fireplace. At the far end of the street, up a turning to the right, is the impressive **Church of St John the Baptist**. Norman works survives in the nave arcades; rather unusually, a thick wall broken only by a small archway separates the nave from the chancel. The remainder of the building is medieval, although the ornate rood screen was made in 1910. There are numerous monuments, including those of two of the village's benefactors, Jerome Poticary, a cloth merchant (1596) and his descendant John Topp, whose canopied tomb (1640) has effigies of Topp, his wife and children.

Opposite the church is a row of 13th-c. *almshouses*.

Stonehenge   4D

Wilts. Prehistoric site off A303, 35m SE of Bath.
Events: Summer Solstice (longest day, Jun); Winter Solstice (shortest day, Dec)

Stonehenge is one of the world's most enigmatic monuments. Speculation continues as to the purpose of the stone circle: whether it served as an astronomical or lunar temple, a centre for sun worship, a Druidic religious centre, a palace or a trade centre. Nor has a satisfactory answer been found to the question of how it was built; suggested explanations have ranged from the use of giant rollers to telekinesis.

What is known is that Stonehenge was not built at one time. Its history covers three distinct periods over nine centuries (2200-1300 BC). Contrary to

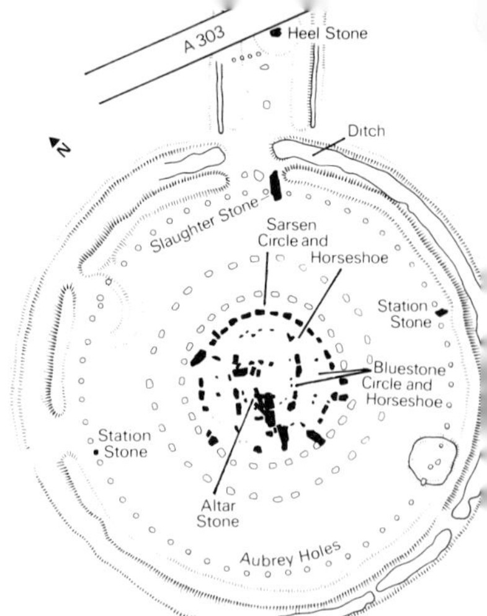

popular belief, the Druids did not build it; they arrived much later. The monument is thought to have been built by the Beaker people, who came over from northern Europe and colonised Britain at the end of the Neolithic period.

As it appears today, Stonehenge is encircled by a low bank 100ft outside the stone circle. Originally about 6ft high and built of chalk rubble, most of the bank has now slipped back into the ditch outlining it. This earthwork is broken by an entrance gap to the NE and by several smaller gaps. From the NE entrance the line of *Stonehenge Avenue*, visible only at its outset, runs down to the River Avon about 2m away. Standing to one side of the avenue, near the road, is the *Heel Stone*, at whose point the sun rises on the longest day or summer solstice.

Inside the bank is a ring of 56 filled-in pits known as the *Aubrey Holes*, after their 17th-c. discoverer John Aubrey. The bank and ditch – together with the Aubrey Holes and the Heel Stone – are the earliest structures, of *c.* 2200 BC. 500 years later, about 80 bluestones, each weighing about 4 tons and believed to have been brought by land and sea from the Preseli mountains of SW Wales, were set up to form a double circle in the centre of the site, with a NE entrance. The avenue was dug at this time – and possibly served as the route along which the bluestones were transported from the river.

The last phase of building took place *c.* 1600 BC. The Early Bronze Age inhabitants of Wessex pulled down the still-unfinished double bluestone circle and set the stone on one side. They then dragged 80 enormous blocks of sarsen stones, known as Grey Wethers, from the Marlborough Downs and set them up in a lintelled *Circle* and a *Horseshoe* of trilithons – the shapes which characterise the site today. Finally they set up the four *Station Stones* (two of which survive at the E and W points of the compass inside the earthwork) and marked the entrance with two more sarsens. Only one of these, the *Slaughter Stone*, remains.

300 years later, the inhabitants formed about 20 of the 80 dismantled bluestones into an oval setting within the Sarsen Horseshoe. These were later reset in the form of the present *Bluestone Horseshoe*. Following this a new *Bluestone Circle* was set up with the Sarsen Circle, using the balance of 60 stones. Only a few of these, and a few of the Bluestone Horseshoe, survive. The largest of the bluestones, the *Altar Stone*, which lies within this horseshoe, has fallen and now lies under a collapsed trilithon.

The axis of the monument, aligned on the Heel Stone, points towards the midsummer sunrise, and, in the opposite direction, to the midwinter sunset. Other astronomical alignments have been found at Stonehenge, one of whose functions may have been to predict eclipses of the sun and moon.

So accurate is the squaring, jointing and placing of the stones that it is believed the people who built Stonehenge were probably influenced by more urban civilisations. Excavations at nearby barrows have unearthed objects imported from the Mediterranean, and carvings of Bronze Age weapons found on the stones can be identified with Mycenaean weapons, suggesting a Mediterranean connection *c.* 1600 BC.

Stourhead (NT) 4B

Historic house and garden off B3092, 10m S of Frome

Stourhead's house and garden give it a double distinction in the heritage of Britain's great country estates. The house, built for Sir Henry Hoare the merchant banker by Colen Campbell in 1721-24, was one of the first in the country in the Palladian style. The garden, laid out for Henry Hoare II by Henry Flitcroft in 1741-50, was one of the first of the new-style English landscape gardens, which replaced the more formal French designs previously in vogue.

Unhappily the central part of the house, Campbell's original work, was destroyed by fire in 1902 and subsequently rebuilt. The two wings added to the house in 1793 survived, as did the W portico (a Campbell design) added in 1840. Most of the ground floor rooms are open to the public. There is some fine furniture, including pieces designed for the house by Thomas Chippendale.

Flitcroft's scheme for Stourhead's gardens transformed a natural valley into a romantic landscape of lakes, grottoes, trees and classical temples, cleverly arranged to create a series of picturesque views. Later planting, particularly of rhododendrons and azaleas, has slightly altered the original concept, but Henry Hoare's vision has been well preserved by later generations of the family. The 6th baronet, Sir Henry Hoare (d. 1947) bequeathed the estate to the National Trust.

Trowbridge 3C

Wilts. Pop. 20,100. 12m SE of Bath (A363). EC Wed MD Tue, Fri & Sat. Inf: Tel (022 14) 63111

Trowbridge is a market town and the county town of Wiltshire. Like Bradford-on-Avon, it was a centre for the cloth industry before Yorkshire took over in the 18th c.

Fore Street is a good central point from which to look round the town. At one end, the junction with Silver Street, stands the late Victorian *Town Hall*, with a plaque commemorating Sir Isaac Pitman (1813-97), inventor of Pitman's shorthand, who was born nearby. There are many fine 18th-c. buildings in Fore Street: note especially the *Midland Bank*. At the other end of Fore Street stands **St James's Church**, a magnificent Perpendicular building endowed by a rich cloth merchant in 1483, and accurately restored in the 19th c. Its tower and spire rise 160 ft. In the chancel is a memorial to the poet George Crabbe (1754-1832) who was a former rector of the church. A window in the Baptistry portrays famous local personalities: Ela, Countess of Salisbury; Queen Philippa; her son, John of Gaunt; and Humphrey de Bohun.

In the churchyard stands a memorial to Thomas Helliker, a cloth finisher executed in 1803 on his 90th birthday for leading riots in protest against the introduction of industrial machinery. He refused to betray his accomplices, who set up the memorial in gratitude.

Urchfont   3D
Wilts. Village off A342, 4m SE of Devizes

A remote, pretty village N of Salisbury Plain built around a small green and duck pond where wild ducks roost. Overlooking the green is the 18th-c. *Manor Farmhouse*, with a Chinoiserie iron porch, and the long, low 14th-c. **Church of St Michael and All Angels**, a cruciform building. Pinnacles adorn both the embattled tower and the vaulted stone porch. The interior is as attractive as the outside, with red-gold stained glass and some interesting monuments. In the chancel stands the tomb of Robert Tothill, Clerk of the Privy Seal to King George II, with busts of Tothill and his wife flanked by weeping *putti* carved by Thomas Scheemakers.

On the W side of the village is *Urchfont Manor*, a late 17th-c. red-brick mansion with later Georgian work added; it is now a residential college.

Wansdyke   2D
This massive earthwork, beginning in Hampshire, stretches 12m across the Marlborough Downs of Wiltshire, then reappears, after a gap, on the Mendip hills. It is thought to have been a Saxon defence system built by slave labour. The name has, in fact, a Saxon origin – Woden's Dyke, or ditch.

The Wiltshire section has a huge bank and ditch on its N side and follows the ridge of the Downs from Savernake Forest to Morgans Hill N of Devizes. On either side, the Downs are dotted with earthworks and hillside forts – at Huish Hill, Knap Hill, Walker's Hill, Milk Hill, Clifford's Hill, All Cannings Down and Horton Down. West Wansdyke can be traced SW of Bath off the A367 near South Stoke; it then reappears at intervals to the NW, ending at Maes Knoll fort N of Stanton Drew.

Warminster   4C
Wilts. Pop 13,500. 21m SW of Bath (A36). EC Wed. Inf: Tel (0985) 212393

Warminster is a busy market town, as well as being the site of the School of Infantry and the workshops of the Royal Electrical and Mechanical Engineers. The town's 18th and 19th-c. houses, shops and inns recall its past prosperity as a wool and coaching centre.

On opposite sides of the Market Place stand *The Bath Arms* and *Old Bell Hotel*, both Georgian coaching inns. Further along is the former *Town Hall*, a 19th-c. building. Nearby is Warminster's oldest building, the **Chapel of St Lawrence**, which has a 14th-c. nave. The tower and spire are 15th-c.; the remainder is Victorian. Nearby, in the High Street, the **Dewey Museum** houses an exhibition of fossils, ancient stones and local history.

Continuing down the hill, along George Street and Silver Street into Church Street, the buildings of **Warminster School** stand on both sides of the road. Built in 1707 in the style of a century earlier, it had as its most distinguished pupil Dr Thomas Arnold, educational pioneer and founder of Rugby School. Nearby stands **St Denys, The Minster**. A 14th-c. cruciform church with a Perpendicular tower, it was heavily restored by Sir Arthur Blomfield in the 1880s. The beautiful organ case inside was originally built for Salisbury Cathedral in 1792.

Warminster offers a choice of open spaces and picnicking spots. Not far from the Market Place, in Weymouth Street, are the *Lake Pleasure Grounds*, with a large boating lake, children's corner, paddling pool and adventure playground. To the N of the town is *Cop Heap*, a conical hill crowned by a beech wood; a huge Bronze Age barrow located there is thought to contain the bones of a Wessex chieftain. The W outskirts of the town are dominated by *Cley Hill* (NT), reputed to be where Alfred the Great camped before he fought against the Danes at the Battle of Ethandune. The hill is now a mecca for spotters of Unidentified Flying Objects, with more authenticated UFO sightings than in any other part of the country.

Wellow 3B
Avon. Village off A367, 8m SW of Bath

The village consists mainly of a long street of 17th and 18th-c. stone cottages. Its most historic possession is the *Maypole* standing in the walled field next to the village school – one of only three permanent maypoles left in England. Once upon a time the wooden pole was renewed regularly; now it has been replaced once and for all by a steel pole. *The Fox and Badger* inn is 16th-c. The late Georgian *Methodist chapel* nearby dates from 1847. A narrow turning leads down from the main street to a picturesque ford and bridge.

At one end of the main street stands **St Julian the Hospitaller's Church**. Dating from the 12th c., it was rebuilt in the 14th c. by Sir Walter Hungerford whose family lived at Farleigh Castle nearby. Over the doorway of the buttressed tower stands a figure of the patron saint. Inside, the richly carved tomb of a lady of the Hungerford family lies beneath an Elizabethan canopy. Nearby lies the much earlier figure of a priest, with a cross cut in his forehead.

½m S of the village stands *Stoney Littleton Long Barrow*, the finest and best-preserved long barrow in the county. Its passage is nearly 50ft long, with three small chambers opening out on either side.

Wells 4A
Somerset Town 21m SW of Bath (A39). Event: Wells Carnival (Nov). EC Wed, MD Wed Sat. Inf: Tel (0749) 72552

England's smallest city has never lost its medieval serenity. The ecclesiastical quarter is shut away from the rest of the city by a series of gates: Chain Gate in the N opening into Vicar's Close, Brown's Gate in the E dividing Cathedral Green from Sadler Street, and Penniless Porch which opens on to Market Place – the natural starting point for a visit to the city.

The Cathedral A church has existed at Wells since the 8th c., when King Ina of the West Saxons founded a place of worship by the spring which gave the city its name. In 1080 the Normans moved the bishopric to Bath. A Bath bishop, Reginald de Bohun, built the core of the present church – the nave, choir, transepts and several chapels – at Wells towards the end of the 12th c., using stone quarried at Doulting. Two of the original chapels, *St Calixtus* and *St Martin*, survive in the present building. Reginald's successor Jocelyn, much to the disapproval of his fellow Bath churchmen, took up residence at Wells, and it was only after years of controversy that his successor, Roger, reached a compromise by styling himself Bishop of Bath *and* Wells. During his term of office Bishop Jocelyn lengthened the nave and built the W front – a spectacular showpiece of English Gothic architecture – consecrating the whole building in 1239. Next to be built was the Chapter House, begun by Bishop Ergum c. 1300, which after the W front is Wells' most memorable feature. The Cathedral was completed before the mid-14th c. with the building of additional chapels, including the Lady Chapel, and the great *Central Tower*. By the end of the 14th c. two towers had been added to the W front: the *Harewell Tower* and the *Bubwith Tower*, named after the bishops who bequeathed them.

The *W Front* is one of the finest in Britain. The 147ft-wide façade contains hundreds of statues of angels, saints,

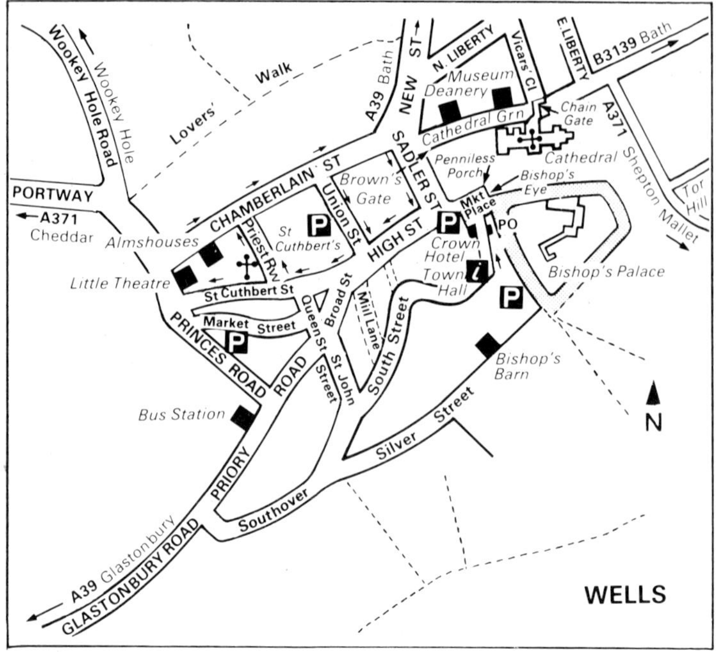

monarchs and bishops; eight projecting buttresses lend further breadth to the design. The great frieze, the greatest gallery of medieval sculpture in Europe, is at present undergoing a thorough restoration.

Entering the Cathedral by the W door, the *nave's* majestic perspective, with its triforium, clerestory and vault soaring above, can be admired for its unity. The unusual inverted arches at the crossing serve to bind rather than disturb this unity: they were inserted to strengthen the central tower, which began to tilt soon after its construction.

The nave has ten bays; of these the four to the E were built by the Cathedral's founder, Bishop Reginald, before the completion of the nave by his successor, Bishop Jocelyn. Reginald also built the superb *N Porch* accessible from the N aisle. The *N transept* has one of the oldest working clocks in the world (1380) – and one of the most en-tertaining. Every ¼hr a tournament of mechanical knights takes place above the clock face, and a seated figure strikes the hour on bells with his hands and feet. This doubles as an astronomical clock, with a 24-hr dial. It also shows the minutes, days of the month and phases of the moon.

The E end of the Cathedral is of particular interest. Like the nave, the *choir* was built in two phases: the first three bays belonging to Bishop Reginald's original 12th-c. building and the rest, beyond the pulpit, the work of a later 14th-c. bishop, Ralph. Above the High Altar is the magnificent 14th-c. *Jesse window*, considered the finest in Britain, and beyond the bishop's throne, between the choir and S choir aisle, is the *Chantry tomb of Bishop Bekynton*, Bishop of Bath and Wells (1443-64) and Chancellor of England. Of the cadaver type, the tomb shows the bishop in his vestments above and his shroud below.

The choir aisles converge behind the High Altar to form the retro-choir. Beyond this is the *Lady Chapel*, with its superb stained glass: that of the N and S windows is 14th-c.

The Cathedral contains many other fine chapels, chantry chapels and tombs commemorating various bishops and notables. The font (*S transept*) is Norman. Access to the Cloister is through the SW tower (souvenir shop).

From the N transept a magnificent curving flight of steps, worn by centuries of use, ascends to the Chapter House. Halfway up, a doorway opens into a gallery, which leads over the Chain Gate to the Vicar's Hall (see below). The octagonal *Chapter House*, one of the architectural splendours of Wells, is built around a central shaft with 18 columns and 30 ribs of vaulting; it contains 51 canopied seats around the walls, each crowned by a carved stone face. Beneath lies the *Undercroft*, originally used as a treasury, with its barred windows and iron-clad double doors.

On the N side of the Cathedral, approached through the 15th-c. *Chain Gate*, is **Vicar's Close**, the oldest inhabited street in western Europe. The precinct was founded by Bishop Ralph in 1348 to house members of the College of Vicars Choral, who were responsible for the administration of the Cathedral. In all there are 42 cells, each with an upstairs and downstairs room and a tiny office. No 22 has been restored to suggest its original condition. Built in the form of an Oxford or Cambridge college quadrangle, the Close lost this appearance when the Vicars asked for gardens in front of their lodgings. At the far end of the Close stands a 15th-c. chapel bequeated by Bishop Bubwith. At the entrance is the *Vicars' Hall*, connected to the Chapter House by the Chain Gate and its bridge. The original panelled dining room with its bay windows and great fireplace may be seen.

Other buildings located on the N side of the Cathedral include the *Canons' Houses* and *Cathedral School*, in the street known as The Liberty, and – opposite the N porch – the *Archdeacon's House* (now the Wells Cathedral School Music School) and the former *Chancellor's House*. The latter building now houses the **Wells Museum and Library**, with exhibitions including the Wookey Hole Cave collection, folk relics, prehistoric pottery and local wildlife displays. Next to the museum is the 15th c. *Deanery*, now Diocesan offices.

From the Cathedral Green, *Penniless Porch* leads through to the Market Place. (The porch, built by Bishop Bekynton in 1450, got its name from its use by the local beggars.) A gate tower to the left, known as *The Bishop's Eye* (built by Bishop Ralph in 1340), gives access to the S side of the Cathedral. Here is the **Cloister** with its splendid *E Walk* donated by Bishop Bubwith in the 15th c. On the floor above is the *Cathedral Library*, whose many rare books and treasures are on display.

Beyond the cloister is the gatehouse leading into the **Bishop's Palace**. The palace, with its picturesque fortifications, moat and drawbridge, was begun in the early 13th c. by Bishop Jocelyn. It is one of the oldest inhabited houses in England: the Bishop of Bath and Wells still resides here.

The oldest part is the house itself (the *Camera*) though much altered in the 19th c. The *Chapel* and *Great Hall* were added by Bishop Burnell towards the end of the 13th c. Parts of the palace were destroyed during the Reformation, and the Great Hall, once used for magnificent banquets, is now a ruin. There is a fine rampart walk, and a view of *St Andrew's Well*, the spring which gave Wells its name.

Near the bridge over the moat a bell is fixed: the swans sometimes ring it for food. Outside the palace, in Silver Street, stands the spacious and heavily buttressed *Bishop's Barn*.

The Borough of Wells Ancient meets modern in the Market Place, where inlaid in the paving stones is a recent memorial to citizen Mary Rand's record-breaking Olympic long-jump.

In the yard behind the 16th-c. *Crown*

Hotel it is said that the persecuted Quaker William Penn – founder of Pennsylvania, USA – preached to a vast crowd before his arrest. The *Town Hall* nearby is Georgian. The medieval water conduit in the middle of the Market Place was rebuilt in 1799.

Down the High Street and to the right, in Priest Row, stands **St Cuthbert's Church**, founded in Saxon times. It has the distinction of being Somerset's largest parish church, and is a particularly splendid example of the Somerset Perpendicular style. Its tower was built in 1430. Inside, the font has a handsome 15th-c. cover. Wells' busy trading life once centred around this church – a fact reflected in the many altars with their various guild associations. In Chamberlain Street, adjoining the church, stand the **Bubwith Almshouses**. These are probably unique in England, being half almshouse and half Guildhall. Their inmates lived in cells in the centre of the buildings, but with the tops of their chambers open so that even when bedridden they might hear the chapel services. Nearby stand more typical almshouses. *Archibald Harpers*, in Chamberlain Street, and *Llewellyns*, in Priest Row, were built especially for the 'poor wool-combers' of Wells' once-flourishing stocking trade.

Walk to Tor Hill (NT) Leave the Market Place by way of the Bishop's Palace gateway. Walk to the E end of the moat, cross the stile, then the road. On the opposite side a winding path leads to the summit. From here there are fine views of the Cathedral and the Bishop's Palace, and in the other direction Glastonbury Tor, the Quantock hills and the Polden range.

Westbury   3C
Wilts. Town 16m SE of Bath (A350).
Event: Festival (Jun/Jul). EC Wed, MD Tue.
Inf. Tel (02214) 63111

Once a busy cloth centre, the town is now well known for the quality of its gloves. A number of Georgian buildings surround the Market Place; note the L-shaped *Lopes Arms Hotel*.

All Saints' Church, although much restored, shows the period of transition between the Decorated and the Perpendicular styles. There is a handsome vault in the two-storeyed S porch. Among the many interesting windows, the baptistry has a stained glass figure of Abraham Laverton of Farleigh Castle. The N transept contains the ornate tomb of Sir James Ley, First Earl of Marlborough, with his wife. One of James I's first knights (1603), he served as Lord Chief Justice and Speaker of the House of Lords.

1½m E of Westbury on the B3098 to Bratton, the famous Westbury *White Horse* can be seen up on the hill. 166ft long and 162ft wide, it was cut in the 18th c. to replace an earlier horse, said to have commemorated King Alfred's defeat of the Danes at Ethandune, 3m away, in 878. Nearby, 4m to the E, is *Bratton Castle*, an Iron Age hill fort. 2m W of Westbury, the **Woodland Park and Phillips Countryside Museum** is made up of 80 acres of forest dating back over thousands of years; it is now run as a commercial forest. There is a 5-acre lake with wild-fowl, as well as a number of forest walks; the museum has displays throughout the year.

West Cranmore   4B
Somerset. Village and museum off A361, 8m SW of Frome

West Cranmore is a railway lover's mecca: the home of the East Somerset Railway. **Cranmore Station**, on the former railway line running between Witham and Shepton Mallet, houses a remarkable collection of steam locomotives, a workshop, and an art gallery in an engine shed. The station is carefully restored down to the last nostalgic advertisement and also contains a remarkable reconstruction of a Victorian engineshed. The station and its collection are the work of artist and steam enthusiast David Shepherd.

The tower of **St Bartholomew's Church** is a 15th-c. replica of the tower at Shepton Mallet – a smaller version crowned with battlements and richly decorated with gargoyles on the cornice. Inside the building a 17th-c. brass commemorates the births of two local residents, James and Amy Strode; there are also memorials to the Bisse family, rich clothiers.

On the hillside N of the village stands *Cranmore Tower*, a folly built by a Mr Paget in 1862; Italianate in style, it has balconies and arching windows.

West Kennet Long Barrow 2D
Wilts. Ancient site off A4, 26m E of Bath

A signposted footpath leads off the main road to the earthwork. The 350 x 75ft barrow was built *c.* 2700 BC and used (though perhaps not built) by the Windmill Hill people, a tribe who migrated from France *c.* 3000 BC. Inside the barrow is the largest chambered tomb in the country. The tomb entrance stands between gigantic upright sarsen stones. A long passage, with two groups of burial chambers opening off it, leads down to a larger chamber at the far end. Over 40 skeletons were found here; finds are on show at Devizes Museum.

E of the Long Barrow stands the ancient man-made mound of *★Silbury Hill*, while NW is the prehistoric stone circle of *★Avebury*, and beyond it, *★Windmill Hill* with its Neolithic earthworks.

Westwood Manor (NT) 3C
Wilts. Historic house and church off A363, 8m SE of Bath

A fine example of a Wiltshire manor house, with gables, dormer windows and rich plaster ceilings. The earliest parts of the house date from *c.* 1400, but what the visitor sees belongs more to the early 16th c. when the clothier Thomas Horton lived here. During the 17th c. a later owner, John Farewell, made a number of alterations. The house has a medieval Great Hall with a chamber above. The King's Room is decorated with painted panel-portraits of 22 English rulers up to the time of Charles I. The Manor has formal topiary gardens.

St Mary's Church nearby is probably of Norman foundation, but was rebuilt in the 15th c. It has an impressive Perpendicular tower, built by Thomas Horton. The stained glass is particularly colourful: a fine example is the E window depicting the Crucifixion. Among the monuments is a tablet to Charles Francklin with an acrostic verse.

Widcombe 2B (Bath area)
Avon. Village off A36 ½m SE of Bath

Once an outlying village, Widcombe is now a suburb of Bath.

A turning up Widcombe Hill leads to *Widcombe Crescent*, designed by Harcourt-Masters in 1805; beyond lies Widcombe Terrace. Continuing along Church Lane, on the right stands *Widcombe Lodge*; here Henry Fielding wrote part of his novel *Tom Jones*, and the poet Walter Savage Landor composed his most famous verse. From here the portico of Prior Park can be seen on its hillside. Further along on the left is the **Church of St Thomas à Becket**; founded in the 12th c., it was rebuilt by Prior Cantlow in the 15th c. The building consists simply of a nave and chancel, with a panelled chancel arch and a roodloft stairway leading to the pulpit. On the wall of the tower hangs a facsimile page from a Saxon Gospel book prepared for the church by the Abbot Brithwolde not later than 983 AD. On another wall there is a brass portrait of Prior Cantlow.

Opposite the church is *Widcombe Manor*, built by Thomas Greenway in 1727. The house has an entrance façade of seven bays and two storeys, with Corinthian pilasters. In the forecourt stands an exquisite bronze late-16th-c. Venetian fountain. *Widcombe Lodge*, next door, was where Henry Fielding wrote his novel *Tom Jones*.

Church Lane, behind the church, leads down past a field to a point where, through a tall gate, there is a good view of Prior Park's Palladian bridge and fish ponds. (See also *Walk 3*, p. 17.)

Windmill Hill (NT) 2D
Wilts. Ancient site off A361 9m NE of Devizes

The down, together with its three concentric lines of Neolithic earthworks dotted about with barrows, has given its name to a tribe who migrated to England from France *c.* 3000 BC. Excavations have shown that the Windmill Hill people were pioneer agriculturalists who grew wheat, barley and flax. They kept sheep, pigs and long-horned cattle; the skeleton of one of their chow-like dogs can be seen at Avebury Museum. Pottery has also been found on the site along with carved ornamental pendants and the remains of small flint axes.

SE of the site is the prehistoric Stone circle of *Avebury* and beyond it, *Silbury Hill* and *West Kennet Long Barrow*.

Woodhenge 4D
Wilts. Ancient site off A345, 39m SE of Bath

Believed to be the prototype of Stonehenge, Woodhenge was discovered in 1925 by a pilot flying overhead. The late Neolithic site consists of an enclosure and timber setting which forms six concentric circles. The positions of the original wooden posts have been marked with concrete posts. Beyond the outer ring can be seen the traces of a ditch and rampart broken by a causeway. Inside the innermost ring is a shallow grave cut 1ft deep in the chalk; here archaeologists found the skeleton of a murdered child. The position of this grave corresponds to the altar stone at Stonehenge. From the site another late Neolithic enclosure, *Durrington Walls*, can be seen away to the N; this huge earthwork consists of a circular bank and ditch about 1700 ft in diameter.

Wookey Hole 3A
Somerset. Stalactite caves off A371, 2m NW of Wells (Wookey Hole Road)

Wookey Hole Caves 25 chambers have so far been discovered here through the work of H.E. Balch and other archaeologists. Of the 25, only nine are accessible to visitors.

The Caves were regularly used by human beings from about 250 BC until 400 AD. Evidence of human sacrifice has been found, which suggests the origin of the 'old witch' legend. Bones of animals – wild horse, fox, deer, woolly rhino, lion, bear, mammoth, hare – found in the Hyaena Den date back to the Old Stone Age (about 50,000 BC), when the animals are thought to have been driven from the glaciers covering the foothills of Wales.

Wookey Hole Paper Mill Paper is known to have been made by hand here in the early 18th c., although the present buildings date back to the mid-19th-c. A watermark was registered for the Mill in 1783. In recent years the Madame Tussauds organisation, which owns the Wookey Hole estate, has restored the beater room, vat house and drying loft to working order. Visitors can now watch paper being made by hand and afterwards buy writing paper and drawing blocks at the Mill shop.

Lady Bangor's Fairground Collection This colourful collection of fairground objects spans the period between 1870 and 1939. It includes a working Marenghi organ, decorative roundabout gallopers, and a host of dolphins, Neptunes, Welsh dragons and other animal carvings produced by craftsmen such as Cernigliano and Anderson.

Madame Tussaud's Store Room Famous and infamous wax heads, plaster negatives for limbs, costumes and props are stored here, sometimes for re-use, sometimes for reference.

Wookey Hole Museum displays not only finds from the caves but also some of the cave divers' equipment.

Walk to Ebbor Gorge (NT) Walk past the cave to the end of the village and take the lane on the right (unsignposted, but known locally as Deer Leap). The road soon becomes very steep. Entrance to the nature reserve is at the top on the right. Two nature trails start from the picnic area on top.

Yarnbury Castle 4D
Wilts. Ancient site off A303, 31m SE of Bath

This Iron Age fort is the second largest prehistoric fortress in Wiltshire after Casterley Camp – and the finest. It has triple ditches, one 50 ft deep, and four ramparts, the central one being the earliest (5th c. BC). When the original entrance was excavated a 12-ft ditch was found, built in a V shape so that attackers could not fight standing one behind the other.